Martín Fierro

Martín Fierro

An Epic of the Argentine

Henry A. Holmes and
José Hernández

MINT EDITIONS

Martín Fierro: An Epic of the Argentine was first published in 1923.

This edition published by Mint Editions 2021.

ISBN 9781513282541 | E-ISBN 9781513287560

Published by Mint Editions®

 MINT
EDITIONS

minteditionbooks.com

Publishing Director: Jennifer Newens
Design & Production: Rachel Lopez Metzger
Project Manager: Micaela Clark
Typesetting: Westchester Publishing Services

To
My Wife

CONTENTS

—

Preface

My acquaintance with *Martín Fierro* dates from November of 1917, when I was living in Montevideo, Uruguay. In Argentina, during the years 1918–1920, I had more than one opportunity of seeing the present-day Argentine plainsmen, and the pampa over which the real *gauchos* had raced their steeds. Of all the themes which a three years' residence in that land of promise suggested to me as worthy of literary treatment, that of *Martín Fierro* has assumed ever more significant proportions, and now I present these cowboys of the South, and their spokesman Martín, to a North American reading public.

I have to thank many friends and acquaintances in the River Plate region, for their assistance in my studies. Professor Ricardo Rojas, of the Buenos Aires University, an authority on Argentine literature, gave me a memorable interview, in which many *Fierro* problems were thoroughly discussed. The treatment of *Martín Fierro* in Rojas' *Historia de la Literatura Argentina* is unsurpassed, and has very considerably influenced me. My friends and assistants in the American College of Buenos Aires, Sr. Pedro D. Viera, and Srta. Emma Day, were most helpful in furnishing material. Professor J. L. Gerig of Columbia University deserves warm thanks, as does also Professor H. A. Todd, not only for his constant encouragement, but also especially for his reading of the book in manuscript and in proof. I cannot be sufficiently grateful to Dr. Federico de Onís, Professor of Spanish Literature in Columbia University, for his suggestions, criticism, and unremitting interest in the work. To my wife, without whose sympathetic co-operation the book probably would never have been written, I thankfully acknowledge my indebtedness. With all its shortcomings, it is an enthusiastic tribute to a land which we both love.

H. A. H.
New York University,
February, 1923

I

The Gaucho

In 1893, at the World's Folk-Lore Congress at Chicago, a brilliant Argentine writer presented a hitherto practically unknown personage to the American public—the *gaucho* of the pampas. Today, to introduce Martín Fierro, counterpart of our North American cowboy of the West, who is the supreme incarnation of the gaucho type, I can do no better than quote, in English translation, the following brief paragraphs from that appreciative address.[1]

"The gaucho is a wanderer, a prodigal son of society. Born in some *rancho* of the Argentine pampa, a branch soon severed from the parent trunk, raised on horseback, he learns from boyhood days to struggle and to suffer. He matures, face to face with impassive nature, holding always this notion: that he should not and cannot rely on anyone but himself alone. . .

"An infinitesimal speck in the midst of that emptiness which for him is the whole universe, like the Mohican (i.e., Uncas, in the novel by Fenimore Cooper) he has every sense sharpened as though it were an indispensable weapon: has acquired the hearing and scent of a wild animal, the keen vision of a falcon; and he likewise possesses that bodily insensibility, that resistance to cold and hunger, that faculty of enduring pain and healing his injuries, characteristic of lower organisms . . .

"He 'hires out' on some *estancia* (great cattle ranch, as we use the term 'ranch'), but almost never for long; since he prefers to wander in quest of festivity, brandings, and races, urged by the incurable desire for adventure and the homesickness for the desert. Indolent and a spendthrift, what money he earns slips through his fingers.

"With all his vices and peccadilloes, one always comes to love him, for he is frank, brave, hospitable, very loyal, and even ingenuous beneath his hirsute exterior."

Sarmiento[2] calls him the "Hawkeye," the "Trapper" of Cooper, with all the frontiersman's knowledge of the plains, with all his aversion to the cities of the white man. "Mysterious personage! his home is on the

---

1. Groussac, *El Gaucho*, in *Viaje Intelectual,* 57 *et passim.*
2. *Facundo,* 77.

pampa... This man is (often) divorced from society and proscribed by law... but he is not a bandit."

Ascasubi,[3] an Argentine poet who knew and loved the typical *gaucho*, thus describes him:

"The gaucho inhabits the Argentine plains: he is an extraordinarily expert horseman, cattleman, and all-round ranchman. As a rule, he is poor, but independent, because of his very poverty and few requirements; he is hospitable, profoundly intelligent and shrewd, physically alert, of few words, wise and energetic in action. In communicating with strangers he shows great caution. In beliefs and language, he has a vast fund of romance and superstitions. Nothing could surpass his ability to traverse alone the immense Argentine deserts, with no other equipment than his lasso and *bolas* (cf. Chapt. VI), obtaining food, horses, and whatever else he may need."

General Mansilla, a soldier and traveller who knew Argentina and the Argentines better than most, has this to say:[4]

"The true gaucho is the wandering creole: a gambler, a fighter, and a foe to all discipline. He flees from compulsory military service when it is his turn, he escapes to the Indians if he stabs anyone, and joins the uprising if there is any to join."

From the foregoing, the reader will understand that the gaucho is neither an artisan nor an artist. His occupation takes him away from cities and the sea. Trade, industry, schools—he is inclined to despise all these. In the first half of the nineteenth century, the Argentine Provinces of Buenos Aires, Santa Fé, Entre Ríos, and Corrientes called the gaucho to essential and often highly specialized tasks. Since good grazing was the rule, the raising of cattle was not merely the occupation of the inhabitants of those provinces, but also their means of subsistence.[5] Those of us who have thrilled at the tale of innumerable buffaloes in the old Far West, or of strenuous days for the cow-punchers on Texas or Wyoming ranches, should be able to imagine the grassy Argentine pampas covered with cattle, horses, and sheep, and enlivened by gaucho centaurs. And externally, the lives of the respective "cowboys" of the two continents were much alike. On the pampas, as in Texas, there were always cattle to brand, grazing to be provided, calves and yearlings to protect, beeves to slaughter,

---

3. *Santos Vega*, 30, Note.
4. Quoted in Garzón's *Diccionario Argentino*, art. *Gaucho*.
5. Sarmiento, *op. cit.*, 55.

horses to tame, sheep to shear and "corral." Where thousands or even scores only of animals were maintained, there was always a demand for dressers of hides, repairers of harness and weapons, builders of houses, walls, and gates. Though the provinces named were then little interested in agriculture, some fields had to be sown, gardens cultivated, ditches and wells dug, and trees saved from the locusts.

But all else pales beside the importance attached to "breaking" horses and coping with wild steers. Here the gaucho truly approved himself. If vaulting ambition spurred him on to strive for further palms, he might become a *baquiano*, or guide-scout, perfectly at home in twenty thousand square leagues of plain, forest, and mountain![6] Such a gaucho was Fructuoso Rivera, an Uruguayan general in the period we are considering; such the far-famed tyrant of Argentina, Juan Manuel Rosas, who could tell in darkest night, by the taste of the grass, to what part of the trackless Buenos Aires pampa he had come. Or our gaucho might aspire to be a *rastreador* or trailer, a human bloodhound, an Argentine Uncas. There was no lack of occupation for gauchos in those brisk days!

Were the gauchos to find themselves always in demand? We shall see! . . .

Nothing more inevitable than that the plainsman should react to his environment. About him stretched the desert. "Everywhere is immensity: immense the plain, immense the forests, gigantic the rivers, the horizon ever misty, mingling with the earth in thin vapors and scudding clouds. Members (sc. of a caravan) involuntarily turn their gaze southward at the slightest whisper of the wind through the dry grass. . . in the deepest shades of night seeking to discern the sinister outlines of savage, stalking hordes."[7]

It would seem that every thought of a being placed in an arena so gigantic, must of necessity be colored, if not suggested, by the sublimity of the scene. But like the sailor, the gaucho has his trivialities. Many, too, of his more serious thoughts were loaded with superstition, distorted by wildest fantasies. Like the animal life by which he was surrounded, he was reared by instinct. And amid these deadly perils, as well as in his stirring daily tasks, the gaucho came to rely upon and love his horse— his unfailing associate, deliverer, friend. Man and beast together lived "close to Nature's heart."

---

6. *Ibid.*, 74.
7. *Ibid.*, 44.

His dealing with elemental forces profoundly affected not only his demeanor and mental states, but also his appearance. Bunge's picture[8] of him emphasizes the influence of environment:

"He was strong and handsome; olive-complexioned, bronzed by the out-of-doors; of medium height; wrinkled as a mystic; with thick, knotted muscles testifying to his rude daily tasks. His piercing black eyes were wont to plumb the depths of desert perspectives. Horsed, he was a centaur. On foot, he made a less striking appearance, having slightly bowed shoulders and crooked legs. His regular features, silky hair and beard, and especially the soft grace of his women-folk, reminded one of the Arab, transplanted to the banks of the Betis."

Nor should we forget the influence of social forces: the townsmen whom the gauchos distrusted, the foreigners whom they despised,[9] their *caudillos* (regional leaders) whom they followed to the death, their Indian foes ever returning from that mysterious Southland, the corrupt officialdom of their limited world, and their women, affectionately nicknamed *chinas* (literally, Indian or half-breed women).

From dictionaries and descriptions, our trail of investigation has led us through geography and sociology, to history and the questions, "Whose son is the gaucho, what, in the historical sense, did he do, and whither did he vanish?"

In answering the first, one is aware of the unalterable dissimilarities existing between the gaucho and our western cowboy. Their tasks might be much alike, their environments even might yield more resemblances than we would at first imagine, but their respective origins fix a great gulf between them, spiritually.

I propose to answer the first question by a selective symposium of the statements of several authorities.

F. M. Page tells us:[10]

"The Indian maiden or matron passed from the *toldo* (tent) of father or husband, into the tent or *rancho* of the white man. The women became willingly and indeed eagerly the wives and concubines of their proud conquerors. Thus originated an incongruous fusion of races,

---

8. Edition of *La Cultura Argentina* of *Martín Fierro*, Introd. ix.

9. Sarmiento, *ibid.*, 61, relates this anecdote: when the French squadron was blockading Buenos Aires, Gen. Mansilla said in the National Congress, "What have these Europeans, who can't stand one night's gallop, to do with us?" And his voice was drowned in the applause of the common people who had thronged to hear him.

10. *Los Payadores Gauchos*, 23.

out of which came especially . . . the gaucho. The type became more decidedly Spanish in proportion to the proximity to the coast."

Leopoldo Lugones:[11]

"Lacking women at first, the conquerors had taken them from the aborigines as they vanquished the latter. . . In the frontier settlements, the lack persisted, and woman continued for a long time to be part of the spoils of war."

Palemón Huergo[12] writes in a newspaper critique:

"Blending their race with that of the aborigines, they (i.e., the Spaniards) originated an intermediate class, the gauchos."

Joaquín M. González[13] writes:

"There would not fail to occur the natural phenomenon of reciprocal influences, which result in the birth of a new soul, heir to the combined physical and psychological characteristics of its progenitors."

Ricardo Rojas[14] declares that the original elements in the South American melting-pot have been the Indian, common all over the continent, and the Spaniard.

Deán Funes of Córdoba, the historian, says:[15]

"This reconciliation was sealed by the marriage of certain Indian women with the Spaniards (Paraguay, 1540). From the union of these two peoples are sprung the *mestizos*" and he continues with observations tending to indicate that the phenomenon was frequent enough.

Pablo Groussac[16] is conservative, but possibly regarding the recent rather than the past generations:

"The gaucho has in his veins only a small quantity of Indian blood. After every generation, this amount is thinned by a richer total of European blood."

C. O. Bunge[17] speaks in two passages, of very infrequent intermingling of *the gaucho and the Indian* (italics mine). But our investigation deals with the *origin* of the gauchos of whom he speaks, not with unions they may have contracted personally.

---

11. *El Payador*, 42–43.
12. In *El Nacional* of Buenos Aires, May 22, 1853.
13. *La Tradioión Nacional*, I, 65.
14. *Historia de la Literatura Argentina*, I, 74.
15. *Ensayo de la Historia Civil de Buenos Aires, Tucumán y Paraguay*, I, 88, 39.
16. *Op. cit.*, 55.
17. *Op. cit.*, Introd. 19 and 32.

To sum up, most of the writers quoted are of the opinion that during the sixteenth and seventeenth centuries, intermarriage was very frequent in the whole River Plate region. The passage quoted from Funes implies it was not infrequent in the eighteenth also. Even in the day of Martín Fierro, unions of white men and Indian women were not uncommon, and the reverse relation was well known in the *tolderías* (Indian villages) after a successful invasion.

It will occur to the reader that a study of the origin of the term 'gaucho' might throw light on his antecedents. But such hopes seem thus far to have proved vain. Groussac insists[18] that the word *gaucho* comes from a contemptuous *gauducho,* which is derived from *gauderio* (cf. vulg. *goderio*), referable, in turn, to Latin *gaudeamus* (!). The form *gauderio* can be traced back historically, he says, as far as 1750. The *gauderios* were happy-go-lucky, thieving, guitar-strumming roamers of the Uruguayan plain, at that time almost a desert solitude. Confidently, then, Groussac pronounces,[19] first, that the gaucho type is originally Uruguayan; secondly, that it did not exist before 1750. Has he forgotten what Deán Funes wrote of old Paraguay?

But the Argentine *romance* with the fairly lengthy title, *Canta un guaso en estilo campestre los triunfos del Excmo. Señor Don Pedro de Cevallos,* which is mentioned in the following chapter, and which uses *guaso* and *guaza* exactly as we say today *gaucho* and *gaucha,*—cannot be later than 1778, and its conception of the *guaso* is evidently not novel. *Guaso,* an Indian word signifying a rustic, reminds us of *guacho,* also an Indian word, meaning illegitimate, or orphan, hence vagabond, and also domesticated. One may suppose that, by an easy metathesis, *guacho* was transformed into *gaucho.* But while some think this theory necessary, in order to explain *gaucho,* others do not.[20] As possibly the least unsatisfactory conclusion, and an offset to the two "positive facts" of Groussac, I offer the following: First, that in the *Argentine pampa* the gaucho type, speaking ethnologically and sociologically, was familiar as early as 1750, if not earlier. Second, that the word *gaucho* was borrowed from the Araucanian or some other Indian tongue, to describe this class of mixed origin, which was so unfortunate.

Nevertheless, the gaucho's record on the pages of earlier Argentine history is far from inglorious. In the troubled days of the seventeenth

---

18. *Op. cit.,* 411–415.

19. *Ibid.,* 413.

20. Cf. Lenz, *Diccionario,* 344, and Bunge, *op. cit.,* Introd. x.

and eighteenth centuries, his fathers and he were holding a few leagues of pampa, close to the Atlantic litoral, against constantly repeated Indian attacks. (Between these struggles, more friendly relations sometimes prevailed, just as later Rosas had an Indian godson,[21] and Mansilla an Indian goddaughter.[22]) Even toward the hostile South, new footholds were ever being made good, by gauchos and other settlers in the Province of Buenos Aires.

The poetry of the War for Independence shows how the fight for colonial expansion had developed self-reliance and intensified the love of freedom in gaucho hearts. When the time came to sever all the oppressive bonds that bound the provinces to Spain, the Argentine gauchos were ready to "do their bit"—which was not a small one. Likewise, the Uruguayan gauchos rallied to Artigas and helped rid their land of the Spanish forces.[23]

"The gaucho," says Rojas,[24] "is the protagonist 'of the Independence,' in Güemes' camp in Salta or in San Martín's in Mendoza; the protagonist of federal democracy with Ramírez . . . and Urquiza; . . . the protagonist of civil expansion out across the pampa, with Rosas. . . and with Roca. Gaucho singers of the pampa. . . were bled white by a century of campaigns, in which the stock succumbed." It is with the last days of the race that our study will have to do.

When the gaucho had outlived his usefulness to his eminently unaltruistic superiors, then "there rose up a new king . . . which knew not Joseph." Sarmiento, President of the Argentine Nation, 1868–74, was not exactly a zealous friend of the gauchos. On the contrary, he appealed most urgently for European immigrants—for throngs of Spaniards and Italians who should develop the untouched resources of a wondrously wealthy land. In desiring the benefits of agricultural development, he was right, and it is with no intent to blame him that I quote from his *Facundo* some closing lines.

"The principal factor contributing to order and stability in the Argentine Republic today is (to be found in) the European immigrants. . . If there existed a government capable of directing them,

---

21. Mansilla: *Una Excursión a los Indios Ranqueles,* 263.
22. *Ibid.,* 8.
23. I might note many another similarity between the Argentine gaucho and his Uruguayan brother, but this study is limited to matters particularly representative of the Argentine side of the Plata.
24. *Op. cit.,* 511.

they in themselves would be sufficient to cure all the wounds inflicted on our land by all the bandits from Facundo to Rosas, in just ten years. . . (Foreseeing that this will actually happen, he continues) That day, the industrious European immigrants will head en masse for the River Plate, and the new administration will see to their distribution through the provinces. . . All the river banks will be covered with cities, and our population will be doubled."[25]

This new administration, then, marked the beginning of the gauchos' gradual disappearance. What were the erstwhile lords of the land to do? Of course, those somewhat imbued with the city training, were able to save themselves from the impending calamity; really, they ceased being true gauchos. Those who remained loyal to their traditions tried to face the storm, but had to succumb.

Out on the sparsely settled pampa, when the first colonizers appeared, the police chiefs and local judges, with low cunning and brutal shrewdness, saw that it would pay them better to be friends with and propitiate the newcomers, than the nomadic gauchos. So we see the judge and the police commissioner frequently in league with the *pulpero*, who, if not a Basque, was likely to be an Italian, and first cousin to the old-time northern saloon-keeper. In the *pulpería* (general store, with bar), the gauchos too often fell—gambled away their all, and the wicked too often plotted against the just.

The clever colonist, of whatever nationality, was quick to observe the plainsmen, reckoned inwardly the value of their horses, their gear, and their unpretentious homes. As likely as not, the gaucho owed all his material well-being to a *patrón* as little versed in business as himself. Naturally, too, the newcomers reasoned how much more profitably they could manage all this, than the gauchos! From cupidity and envy, it was no long step to violence and fraud, as we shall see. In such crimes not alone the pushing colonist but also the unscrupulous Argentine found profit. Officials frequently shared in the plunder. Similar wrongs have been done the Indian in many parts of our own land. And the historian feels divided in his mind between admiration for the prosperity and development that have arisen from the ashes of the old order, and regret for the loss of all that was picturesque and humanly attractive in it.

"Who knows whither the clouds have fled?" Some of the gauchos filled the obscure graves of Indian warfare. Others fell by the hands

---

25. *Op. cit.*, 344, 346.

of fellow-gauchos. Many, drifting either to capital or distant province, never again appeared on the pampa horizon. Many others ate their hearts out, brooding over the past. Their offspring intermarried with the children of the immigrants, or with the dwellers in cities. Themselves metamorphosed, they looked upon a new pampa, dotted everywhere with bustling towns, crossed by irrigating canals and shining bands of steel, feeding the nations from her ample granaries. And this pampa, not an unnaturally stern parent but rather a titanic power forever deaf to puny man's happiness or despair, calmly reclothes herself from year to year with verdure the richer and grain the more golden, since with her soil has been mingled the dust of those who delighted to call themselves, through good fortune and ill, "the sons of the pampa."

II

A Survey of Argentine Gaucho Literature

The Predecessors of José Hernández

A class which has affected not a little the national destinies and which though outwardly dead still lives in the Argentine consciousness, could hardly fail to leave some literary monuments. Long is the line of writings, much longer that of orally transmitted lyrics, which attest the activity of the Muse in Gaucholand. I refer not solely to the inherently gaucho works; there is an intimate relationship between some of these latter and the writings of men who were not themselves direct representatives of the gauchos, but who sympathized with them and had imbibed their spirit. Only a narrow criticism would exclude works of the second class from what I inclusively term gaucho literature.

The most significant chronological links in the chain of gaucho literature are the following:[1]

1. Anonymous popular lyrics: *coplas, décimas, cielos* and other dance forms, *romances* and dramas.
2. The *romances* of Pantaleón Rivarola (*circa* 1806).
3. The dialogues of Bartolomé Hidalgo (*circa* 1820).
4. Some of the verse of Juan Godoy (1825–64).
5. The *Cautiva* of Esteban Echeverría (1837).
6. The works of Hilario Ascasubi (1830–1872).
7. The *Fausto* of Estanislao del Campo (1870).
8. The *Martín Fierro* of José Hernández (1872, 1878).
9. The *Santos Vega* of Rafael Obligado (1885–1906).
10. Gaucho novels by Eduardo Gutiérrez and others (1880–).
11. Gaucho plays, not isolated as in the case of the dramas mentioned under No. 1, but a regularly evolved and fully developed genre (1884–).

---

1. Bartolomé Mitre's *Armonías de la Pampa*, in *Rimas*, may be considered a refined but distant cousin of the *Martín Fierro* type. Such poems as the hackneyed *El ombú* by Luis Domínguez (1810), and *A mi caballo* by Juan María Gutiérrez (1809–1878) were perfectly familiar, but without inspiration for such writers as Hernández.

The number of the old lyrics which gradually acquired epic characteristics, is well nigh infinite. They are so unique, so redolent of the same atmosphere that is breathed in *Martín Fierro*, that a few lines will suffice to fix the type in mind. Take this anonymous *cuarteta*:[2]

> *Arequipa ha dado el sí,*
> *La Indiecita seguirá;*
> *La Zamba vieja ¿qué hará?*
> *Sufrir jeringas de ají.*

—Zeballos: *Cancionero Popular*, 165–6

These lines occur in *décimas* of great spirit. The associations are epic, if not the form, for those were the days of the continental war for independence.

Or, take from certain *Glosas en Décimas* the following *cuarteta* formed by the last lines of each *décima*:[3]

> *La Patria hoy todo lo puede*
> *Que su rival pereció*
> *Y asciende llena de gloria*
> *A la esfera de Nación.*

—*Ibid.*, 205–206

This exalted sentiment is likewise that of the epic days of Bolívar and San Martín.

When—in the second quarter of the last century—the "Rosistas" were besieging Montevideo, or taking the field against the troublesome Lavalle, both sides, the Federals of Rosas and the Unitarians their opponents, made their lyrics into battlecries, charging these with epic significance.

---

2.   *Arequipa has consented (i.e., to fight for liberty),*
        Indian Cuzco will follow suit.
        And old Lima, what will she do?
        Submit to taking pepper clysters.

3.   *Today the Fatherland is allpowerful,*
        Now that its rival has perished,
        And ascends crowned with glory
        To the position of a Nation.

Ascasubi, whom we shall presently study, contributed numbers of *trovas* (metrical compositions) to the Unitarian cause. A recent parallel occurred in the days when the "Old Contemptibles" were retreating from Belgium into France, and Tommy Atkins made "Tipperary" part of an epic military resistance which has not yet found an adequate bard.

When the gaucho *vihuela* (guitar) was tuned to one or another thrillingly patriotic lay, quite ordinary song-forms were on the way to render homage to Calliope. The same may be observed of the dance music of those times (1830–1852). Merry rural *cielo* or *cielito, media caña,* and *huella* (names of dances) became suddenly as stirring and meaningful as ever "Yankee Doodle" was. The history of a generation may be read in some of them.

A *cielo* which shows admirably the potentialities latent in all these forms, is that entitled *Cielito a la venida de la expedición española al Río de la Plata*.[4] Briefly, the *cielo* was thus performed: five couples joined hands to make a circle, within which a sixth pair executed figures. The gallant sang, and his lady responded. Hence, for vocal purposes, the effect is of stanzas and choruses alternating, with each pair distinct; that is, stanza 1 and its chorus were unlike any other set of stanza and chorus.[5]

> *Cielito, cielo, sí!*
> *(This is lyric.)*
> *Eche un trago, amigo Andrés*
> *(Epic. Cf. requests for wine in the* Cid, *etc.)*
> *Para componer el pecho,*
> *(Epic.)*
> *Y después te cantaré.*
> *(Epic or lyric.)*
>
> —*Ibid.*, 237

There is no fixed scheme of assonance through most of this *cielito*— which is only secondarily a dance-accompaniment—but it is interesting

---

4. *Ibid.*, 237 ff.
5.
> *Cielito, cielo,* yes!
> *Pour me three fingers, friend Andrew,*
> *To mend my lungs,*
> *And then I'll sing for you.*

that the last two choruses should be "renewed forms of the pure *romance,*" in which such poets "created the vigorous epic poetry of our plains."[6] The poetic author[7] was carried away by the spirit of his *cantar de gesta.* We must love him perforce,—he is so devoted to his theme, so beautifully artless, so spontaneous! In three other poems which I shall presently comment upon, these traits are even more pronounced. The epic note is high, clear, and long.

There are preserved to us some Argentine *romances*[8] of the pre-Independence and Independence periods. In the colony and young republic, there must have been a variegated collection of *romances,* but unfortunately, we have lost very many. Probably in Argentina, as in Spain, after the fifteenth century, there had been much lyric and little epic material in these *romances,* but now we are to witness a rebirth of the heroic content, in the *romance* versification. "This. . . variety. . . reaches *wild sublimity* when the *national soul feels the impulse of rebellion.*"[9]

One fairly early *romance, Canta un guaso. . . los triunfos de. . . Cevallos,* early for Argentine history, is thoroughly discussed by Rojas.[10] Probably it was written by Maziel, about 1778. The energetic measures of the Spanish Viceroy, Cevallos, against the Portuguese, across the Plata from Buenos Aires, form the subject of verses wherein gaucho expressions bring us an agreeable though rustic perfume.

Another, anonymous, like most of those I have thus far cited, is entitled *Principio y Fin del Rico y Pobre Sancho Crespín.* There is the merit of patriotism in the following:[11]

---

6. Rojas, *op. cit.,* 277.

7. Probably Hidalgo.

8. I do not propose to enter into a comparison of gaucho poetry with old Spanish *romances.* Cf. Zeballos, *op. cit.,* 244 n., where he unhesitatingly puts Hidalgo among the *romanceros,* thereby implying for all poetry like Hidalgo's dialogues, kinship with the Spanish *romances.*

9. García Velloso: *Historia de la Literatura Argentina,* 886.

10. *Op. cit.,* 330.

11.   *Then came the hero, God protect him!*
          For our defense,
          The unconquered San Martín,
          Worthy of eternal fame.
          With the fear his sword inspired—
          With his triumphant presence,
          The tyrant's hordes
          Fled in panic.

Vino el héroe, que Dios guarde,
Para la defensa nuestra,
El invicto San Martín,
Digno de memoria eterna.
Con el temor de su espada,
Con su triunfante presencia
La chusma de los tiranos
Despavorida se ahuyenta.

—*Cancionero Popular,* 269–271

However, this is not typical gaucho talk.

I should not forget to include among the anonymous works, *El amor de la estanciera,* 1792, a drama, full of gaucho scenes. Probably it was not the only one of its kind.

For other *romances,* the reader is referred to the *Romancerillo* of Ciro Bayo, or to the examples given in Rojas,[12] or to the *Cancionero Popular* of Zeballos. Numbers IV and V of the latter, written by Don Pantaleón Rivarola, sing of the defense of Buenos Aires against the British Expeditionary Force, in 1806. These are not at all gaucho poems. Neither do they pertain to any branch of what the French call *la grande poésie.* But they are humble and useful little narratives, lowly members of that same clan to which belong the *cantares de gesta.* For the same spirit engenders both.[13]

Una columna va entrando
Que era como de ochocientos,
Cuando de improviso rompen
Entre los nuestros el fuego,
Con tal viveza y tal brío,
Con tal braveza y denuedo

---

12. *Op. cit.,* 313–315.

13.
A column is entering
About eight hundred strong,
When suddenly...
Some of ours start firing
With such ardor, such vigor,
With such valor and resolution,
That in a very little while
They cut the column to pieces.

HENRY A. HOLMES AND JOSÉ HERNÁNDEZ

Que en un espacio muy corto,
Destrozaron la columna.

—*Cancionero Popular,* 22

But more interesting to us than these straightforward lines, is the comment made by Rivarola himself upon his *romances:*[14]

"But I shall be asked why, once I had resolved to write the narrative in verse, I did not write in *heroic verse,* like others? First, I write in current verse, because this class of meter is the best adapted to *the songs sung to our common instruments* (italics mine), and consequently the one most appropriate for reciting and singing by all kinds of people." Elsewhere he says: "I won't give my name, for I seek not my glory, but God's."[15]

The *romance* was evidently on the lips of ordinary folk, and could be depended upon to sing of themes of supreme national interest. Further, we need not concern ourselves. Whatever *payador* (gaucho bard) we may find constructing a work with epic marks, we are to think of him as not having burst into this domain like some new planet. He is in the succession of Argentine rhapsodists, of whom most are for all time anonymous, some almost so, and some few known and discussed by us here. One bard may write of the desert, the gauchos, and the Indians, where another perhaps wrote of the city and the English invaders, but both yield allegiance to the people's cause, and both conceive a popular song and dance meter to be a thoroughly suitable vehicle for carrying a heroic theme.

In its direct bearing upon *Martín Fierro,* the poetry of Bartolomé Hidalgo (b. 1788—d. 1823) is vastly more important. He was a native of Montevideo, but spent the latter part of his too brief existence in Argentina. He was killed in a skirmish in one of the frequent civil upheavals. Hidalgo essayed to write various forms of verse, but succeeded in two only, the *cielitos* and the dialogues. These latter are not conversations in the ordinary sense, but rather recitals of historic events, past or present, marked by a high purpose and an epic amplitude, and written in octosyllabics. It is great praise that we give him, when we recognize his conquest of this popular verse for more sustained and substantial purposes.

---

14. Quoted in Rojas, *op. cit.,* 321.
15. Prologue to the Second Romance.

Hidalgo's dialogues are in truth *romances*. In them lies a partial explanation of the rise of the great gaucho trio, Ascasubi, Del Campo, and Hernández. Says Menéndez y Pelayo:[16] "It cannot be denied that Hidalgo's dialogues were the source of that peculiar gaucho literature which. . . has produced the most original works in South American literature."

In the first dialogue (1820), the interlocutors, Jacinto Chano and Ramón Contreras, gauchos both, lament the sad falling-off of real democracy and impartial justice, since the good old days when independence was won. The dialogue concludes:[17]

> *Que el que la hizo la pague,*
> . . . .
> *Guerra eterna a la discordia. . .*
> *Y gozaremos el don*
> *Más precioso de la tierra*
> *Americanos, unión.*
>
> —*Cancionero Popular,* 250

Rojas[18] admires the force and fire in Hidalgo's verse, asserting that even Hernández does not achieve such success as that of Hidalgo in the *Cielito a la venida de la expedición española,*[19] save in certain passages. For instance, Chano's restraint in the second dialogue is most commendable. He regrets the lack of union among the patriots, a source of joy to the Spaniards. But he does not dilate on this, and what he says is enlivened by such effective transitions as:[20]

---

16. *Historia de la Poesía Hispano-Americana,* II, 469.

17.
> *Let him who is to blame, pay,*
> . . . .
> *Eternal war upon discord*
> . . . .
> *And we'll enjoy*
> *Earth's most precious gift,*
> *Americans, union!*

18. *Op. cit.,* 273–293.

19. In their collection of popular songs both Zeballos and Carranza ascribe this *cielo* to Hidalgo. But absolute proof of authorship is lacking.

20.
> *Ah! friend, the precious blood*
> *That has been spilt so lavishly!*

Ah! sangre, amigo, preciosa
Tanta que se ha derramado!

—*Cancionero Popular,* 253

The hopes centered in San Martín's Peruvian campaign are dwelt on. Then with another of those characteristically rapid turns, Hidalgo brings us to his conclusion: *ha de cambiar nuestro estado* (our state is bound to change). If José Hernández could have preached all his sermons with equal agility and conciseness, *Martín Fierro* would be even superior to what it is. Before they finish, however, Chano and his *aparcero* (comrade) have given us a most animated account of how the Spaniards were beaten by the patriots, at Chacabuco, Maipo, and elsewhere. Hernández doubtless knew well this tale of Hidalgo's.

The third dialogue turns on a visit one of these worthies had made to the capital, on the anniversary of Independence Day, May 25th. The patriotic fervor is touching. José Hernández had this poem in mind when he wrote to his publishers: "Martín Fierro doesn't go to the city in order to be able to tell his friends later what he has seen on the 25th of May or other like celebration, tales some of which, like the *Fausto,* are certainly very meritorious, but—"[21]

Hernández not merely knew the phraseology used by Hidalgo, but he employed that phraseology himself to make Martín Fierro's tale more realistic. Why should he not employ it? It was common gaucho property. No one would blame an author today for weaving Biblical phrases into his story. However, he takes nothing from the first of the dialogues. We are merely reminded of Hidalgo, here and there. Study the respective passages in parallel columns.[22]

---

21. In Introd. to Edition of 1894.

22.

HIDALGO	HERNÁNDEZ
First Dialogue	*Martín Fierro*
But while the poor man perishes	If she did n't have a copper
From hunger's rigor. . . and	Left, but only a swarm of
Prostitution is coming to	Children, what
Tempt his unhappy widow, who	Else could the poor creature
In her bitter grief sees	Do, in order not to starve?
The sufferings of her little ones.	

HIDALGO	HERNÁNDEZ
First Dialogue	*Martín Fierro*
Pero en tanto que al rigor	Si no le quedó ni un cobre,
Del hambre perece el pobre,	Sino de hijos un enjambre,
. . . .	Qué más iba a hacer la pobre
Y que la prostitución	Para no morirse de hambre?
Se acerca a la infeliz viuda	—*Ida*, VI*
Que mira con cruel dolor	
Padecer a sus hijuelos.	
—*Cancionero Popular*, 249	
Los otros, cual más, cual menos,	Cual más, cual menos, los criollos
Sufren el mismo rigor.	Saben lo que es amargura.
—*Ibid.*, 248	—*Vu*, VII
Roba un gaucho unas espuelas	Pues si usté pisa en su rancho
O quitó algún mancarrón	Lo caza lo mesmo que ave
. . . .	. . . .
Lo prienden, me lo enchalecan,	Y después dicen que es malo
. . . .	El gaucho si los pelea.
Y de malo y saltiador	. . . .
Me lo tratan, y a un presidio	Le amarran codo con codo
Lo mandan con calzador.	Y pa el cepo lo enderiezan.
—*Ibid.*, 250	—*Ida*, II

The others, some more, some less,	Some more, some less, the peasants
Suffer the same hardships.	Know what bitterness is.
Let a gaucho steal some spurs,	Why, if you step inside your ranch
Or run away with a worthless horse	. . . .
. . . .	You are hunted as they hunt birds.
They take him, they bind him,	. . . .
They treat him as a highwayman	Then they say you are bad
And to a prison	If, gaucho-like, you show a fight
They send him, in a tight leash.	. . . .
	They tie one elbow to the other
	And off you go to the stocks.

* Since Part I of *Martín Fierro* is popularly called *La Ida de Martín Fierro*, the abbreviation *Ida* will be employed throughout this work to refer to Part I; similarly, *Vu* will be employed to signify Part II, *La Vuelta de Martín Fierro*. Roman numerals will refer to cantos.

This "reminder" is the more forcible, in that the two bards treat the same social theme. Hidalgo provides a companion for Jacinto Chano, just as later we shall see Hernández provide Fierro with am *amigazo* (good friend), Cruz. This comradeship is of the very essence of the ballad. Hernández was merely later than Hidalgo in employing it.

Between certain verses in the second dialogue, and certain verses of *Martín Fierro* there are unmistakeable likenesses. Here is evidence that Hernández knew—had absorbed, made his own—the poetry of his predecessor:[23]

<table>
<tr><td align="center">HIDALGO
Second Dialogue</td><td align="center">HERNÁNDEZ
Martín Fierro</td></tr>
<tr><td>Nos golpiamos en la boca
Y ya nos entreveramos:
Y a este quiero, este no quiero
Los fuimos arrinconando . . .
—*Cancionero Popular*, 252</td><td>Y golpiándose en la boca
Hicieron fila adelante
. . . .
Como una luz de lijeros—
Hicieron el entrevero
Y en aquella mescolanza,
Este quiero, este no quiero
Nos escojían con la lanza.
—*Ida*, III</td></tr>
<tr><td>¿Quién nos mojaría la oreja
Si unieramos nuestros brazos?
Mas ni todos los tiranos</td><td>Si Cruz hubiera vivido
No habría tenido cuidado,
. . . .</td></tr>
</table>

23.
<table>
<tr><td align="center">HIDALGO
Second Dialogue</td><td align="center">HERNÁNDEZ
Martín Fierro</td></tr>
<tr><td>We beat our palms on our mouths
And now we were in the shock:
And, "take this, leave that,"
We hurled them back. . .</td><td>And beating their palms on their mouths
Their line charged upon us.
. . . .
Like the light for speed
They delivered their shock.
And in that mix-up
"Take this, leave that,"
They picked us out for spearing.</td></tr>
<tr><td align="center">HIDALGO

Who would wet our ear
Should we once unite?
Not all the tyrants together
Had been able to oppress us.</td><td align="center">HERNÁNDEZ

If Cruz had lived,
I would n't have cared. . .
Between us, we'd have offered fight,
I say not to one Indian, but the tribe!</td></tr>
</table>

Juntos. . . .
Nos habían de hacer roncha.
—*Ibid.*, 253

Entre dos, no digo a un pampa,
A la tribu si se ofrece.
—*Vu*, IX

Again and again in the rush of Hernández' story, a word, a phrase, a hint makes us think of the crowded pages of Hidalgo, who of course enjoyed painting leisurely, in purest gaucho language, the plainsmen galloping, or *mateando* (taking *mate*, the Paraguayan tea), or eating roast meat cooked over the open fire, or acting in any one of a dozen other characteristic rôles.

Rojas[24] would have us perceive in the uncertainties connected with the authorship of certain *cielos*,[25] another proof of the really popular nature of Hidalgo's poetry, if it be his.

But most of this is unfortunately scattered and gone. I have referred to some works of his which stand just on the border-line between the anonymous productions of gaucho poetry, and those whose authorship is established. With these uncertainties, Hidalgo must always remain for us less of a flesh-and-blood writer than Hernández, the well-known author of the 'seventies.

El Comercio of Valparaiso, Chile, a sheet then edited by J. M. Gutiérrez, said that Hidalgo had been the founder of the Argentine eclogue. Such praise is not adequate. He found a body of lyric; he left an earnest of the epic which the national consciousness might yet create. Thus he paved the way for Hernández, who, on the whole, surpassed him in the use of popular forms. But in his day, Hidalgo ranked among the first literary men.

Juan Gualberto Godoy (b. in Mendoza 1793, d. there 1864) wrote numerous *romances* in gaucho style, in the same period (1825–64), when he was launching his political diatribes, now at Rosas, now at some other *caudillo*. He is decidedly inferior to Hidalgo. But he keeps alive the poetry *à thèse* which is later such a weapon in the hands of José Hernández. This smacks of the pampa, we say to ourselves of his style, as he attacks that abuse of the peasants' franchises, which later was condemned by Hernández also. The "bosses" thought they could impose their will on the gauchos when election day came. Godoy opens their eyes in the following *décima*:[26]

---

24. *Op. cit.*, 304, 305.
25. *Cancionero Popular*, Nos. 81 and 104.
26.
>   *We've got to obey them*
>   *In matters of the service;*

Esteban Echeverría was born in Buenos Aires in 1805, journeyed to Paris when but twenty years old, was there thoroughly converted to Romanticism, returned in 1830 to Argentina, wrote *La Cautiva* (1837), founded the "Association of May," went into exile because of Rosas, and died early in 1851. Of all his writings, *La Cautiva* is the sole one that claims our attention, largely because it is conceived and executed in the spirit which led Echeverría to say: "The desert is our richest inheritance and we should labor to extract from its recesses... poetry to delight us morally and build up our literature." His fame, says Rojas,[27] lies in having been the first to compose a poem with a "pampean" argument *in cultured style*. For precisely that reason, it is unnecessary to make more than a cursory examination of *La Cautiva*.

Here is a synopsis of the work:

Brian and María, husband and wife, have been carried away captives by the Indians in the course of a successful *malón*, or foray. They flee from the Indian encampment the night their captors hold the customary revel. The escape is largely due to the dauntless heroism of María, but they are unable to withstand the horrors of their return through the desert: pampa fires, hunger, thirst, wild beasts, rivers. Both succumb at the journey's end.

The poem is turgidly romantic, as Echeverría had conceived romanticism during his years in Paris. Explicit where it should rely on intuition, it frequently blunders in description, and always strains after effect. Yet it is meritorious. As in *Martín Fierro,* the desert is the gaucho's antagonist. The great superiority of Hernández consists in

---

27. *Op. cit.*, 423.

that he *is* the gaucho, living his hardships on the printed page, while Echeverría writes *about* the whites, and the Indians, and the pampa, and we feel nothing. Hernández is not indebted to Echeverría, unless it be for inspiration in the dignity, not without charm, with which the latter clothed the pampa. We must limit ourselves here to a very few lines from *La Cautiva*:[28]

> *Oid! ya se acerca el bando*
> *de salvajes atronando*
> *Todo el campo convecino;*
> *Mirad!—como torbellino*
> *Hiende el espacio veloz*
> *El fiero ímpetu no enfrena*
> *Del bruto que arroja espuma.*
> *Vaga al viento su melena*
> *Y con ligereza suma*
> *Pasa en ademán atroz.*
>
> . . . .
>
> *Ved! que las puntas ufanas*
> *De sus lanzas por despojos*
> *Llevan cabezas humanas,*
> *Cuyos inflamados ojos*
> *Respiran aún furor.*
>
> —Canto I

28.
> *Hark! now approaches the band*
> *Of savages, stunning*
> *All the plain about:*
> *See! like whirlwind*
> *Parting rapidly the air*
> *He checks not the furious dash*
> *Of his foaming steed.*
> *His locks float in the breeze,*
> *And at top speed he passes*
> *With fiendish gesture.*
>
> . . . .
>
> *See! the exculting lances*
> *Carry on their points for spoil*
> *Human heads, whose inflamed eyes*
> *Still tell of war's fury.*

The foregoing are some of the horrors of the Indian foray. Fierro also describes one,[29] and we are almost swept off our feet by its rush and brutal force, but we read *La Cautiva* without one hurried breath. The two poems are simply not in the same class. The latter treats of the pampa, but it is not a gaucho poem. *Martín Fierro* most emphatically is. Therefore, we need make no comparison between Hernández and Echeverría, but let it not be forgotten that the latter introduced the Argentine desert into the poetry of Argentina, and that he was sufficiently esteemed to leave behind him a "school" of young writers professing loyalty to his ideals.

Hilario Ascasubi was born in Fray Bentos, in the province of Córdoba, in 1807. During Rosas' dictatorship, he gave the unstinted allegiance of his gaucho muse to the foes of that tyrant. We see him later in Paris, ending (1872) his collected works. He returned to Buenos Aires, and died there in 1875.

Ascasubi was the disciple of Hidalgo. He sometimes names the characters in his *Trovas*, "Jacinto Cielo", and "Ramón Contreras".[30] But if Ascasubi had only written his *Paulino Lucero* and *Aniceto el Gallo*, he would not have had a very direct influence upon Hernández. These poems are so political, so narrowly contemporary, that only by a strong effort of imagination can they be made to live again today, and the same objection must have applied to a considerable degree in 1872, when Hernández wrote. Bear in mind, too, that Ascasubi attacked with the most deadly irony, the very party for which Hernández fought: the Federals and their unique leader, Rosas.

But the most important work of Ascasubi was neither stale, flat, nor unprofitable for Don José. I refer to *Santos Vega o Los Mellizos de la Flor*, first published in Montevideo in 1851, and later greatly enlarged for the definitive edition of Ascasubi's works which Dupont published in Paris in 1872.

The slender plot of *Santos Vega* falls into two divisions: 1. The *payador* Santos Vega enjoys for several days the hospitality of the gaucho Rufo Tolosa and his wife Juana Petrona. To repay it, he relates to them: 2. The story of twin boys (*mellizos*) who were brought up on the *estancia La Flor* at Chascomús, south of Buenos Aires, in the closing years of the eighteenth century. One of them, ungrateful, crafty, and desperately wicked, stalks

---

29. *Ida*, III.
30. Cf. *Paulino Lucero*, 230–251.

through the story doing all the evil an outlaw gaucho can do, and dies at the very close of the book, by a manifest display of divine justice.

The story is nothing. But what the author terms "dramatic features of gaucho life out on the plains," is exceedingly picturesque and is illuminated by his own notes. This *romance* makes it evident that the technique of gaucho poetry has progressed since the days of Hidalgo. Not that he is inferior to Ascasubi; but the field has been enriched. Hernández will finally inherit all these accretions.[31]

Ascasubi bequeathed to his literary successors the example and stimulus of a lengthy *romance* on gaucho life, and his expert use of gaucho terminology. Moreover, Ascasubi—reinforced, it is true, by Mitre and Obligado—made Santos Vega a sort of tutelar deity of the gaucho bards and the Argentine lyric in general. The poem of *Martín Fierro* gained by all this, as Martín too was a *payador*, whom we shall fail to understand if we do not endow him with the mantles of Vega and Chano and Contreras and their like.

Ascasubi helped to fix the type of the gaucho outlaw.

Also, though this takes us away from *Santos Vega*, Ascasubi sang against Rosas in *trovas* after the gauchos' own hearts. The example of his lampooning proved irresistible to Hernández. Less buffoonery he has, perhaps, but no less energy, as witness his plain words about unjust judges.

An examination of kindred passages dealing with Indian invasions and outlaw fights with police platoons, will show how differently Ascasubi and Hernández worked out the same commonplace themes of frontier life.[32]

---

31. It is true that for Part I of *Martín Fierro*, only two fifths of *Santos Vega*, as we have it today, could have been in any sense a model. The other three fifths were known to Hernández after he published his Part I, but in those three fifths, there is many a cumbersome line, as in Part II of *Martín Fierro*.

32.   THE INDIAN ATTACK

ASCASUBI	HERNÁNDEZ
They charge uttering yells,	And beating their palms on their
In half-moon formation	mouths
. . . .	Their line charged upon us
Like echoes of hell	. . . .
Resound, hoarse and confused,	What yelling! what a din!
Rude trumpets of hide	How they spurred in mad career!
. . . .	The whole tribe united
So when they engaged in battle	Charged with wild yells

With the Christians, if perchance
In the first cannon-volley
Three or four Indians bite the dust,
The rest flee like rising vapors;
And at the clink of swords
Their women as they escape
Begin straightway to drop
Their little ones behind them.
But when in triumph
They return from the fray,
They leave the towns in ashes
'Mid yet other horrors.
And appeals for mercy go unheard,
For they make their onset blindly.

The devils! . . . had us already
    rushed
Like a wild horse troop
. . . .
Came an Indian foaming,
Stretched out on his horse's side,
Whirling overarm
His lance, as one speeds a lasso,
And shrieking closed with me
. . . .
Out came my trusty *bolas*
And I played him to my horse's
    boundings. . .
Till at last with a hit
Of the *bolas*, I brought him down.

The Fight with the Gendarmes

Ascasubi

. . . and he (i.e., Genaro) cast
The *bolas* so skilfully
That by the throw he bound them
Around the legs of the horse,
In such wise that there he fell,
Tossing the gaucho o'er his head
In a whirling fall
The villain was instantly on foot,
So agile was he,
And thinking to resist,
Had recourse to his pistol;
But as he essayed to cock it,
Just then the hammer fell:
And then he wanted to draw
His sword from the saddle-pads,
But Genaro gave him no time,
Stood over him, with the musket,
Said: "Down, thief, face to the ground!
Quick! Else I'll not leave you sick,
But dead, by God and my
blunder-buss!"

Hernández

Every mother's son rushed me
Where I stood ready for them,
. . . .
I gave a spring and fearlessly
Mixed in their very midst
. . . .
The daintiest chap
Stood up to me with a cut,
. . . .
Before he could step in
I threw dust in his eyes!
. . . .
But. . . in my ribs. . . ha! I feel
The fearsome tickling of cold steel!
. . . .
I took a step or two back
Until I got my distance,
Drove one 'fore me, point and edge!
Till a hole brought him stumbling
    down
And down I sent him—to the pit!
(Unexpectedly, the police sergeant
turns his ally.)
One of two foes he sent to hell.
The rest recoiled—we were going strong!
In a trice they were off,
Hopping as fast as any flea!

The Indian Attack

ASCASUBI	HERNÁNDEZ
Cargan pegando alaridos	Y golpiándose en la boca
Y en media luna formaos	Hicieron fila adelante
. . . .	. . . .
Y como ecos del infierno	¡Qué vocerío! ¡qué barullo!
Suenan roncas y confusas	¡Qué apurar esa carrera!
Rudas trompetas de cuerno	La indiada todita entera
. . . .	Dando alaridos cargó
Ansí que cuando pelean	Jué pucha. . . y ya nos sacó
Con los cristianos, que acaso	Como yeguada matrera
En el primer cañonazo	. . . .
Tres o cuatro indios voltean,	Vino un indio echando espuma,
Juyen como exhalaciones;	. . . .
Y al ruido de los latones,	Tendido en el costillar
Las chinas al disparar,	Cimbrando por sobre el brazo
Empiezan luego a tirar	Una lanza como un lazo
Al suelo pichigotones.	Me atropelló dando gritos—
Pero cuando vencedores	. . . .
Salen ellos de la empresa,	Desaté las tres marías
Los pueblos hechos pavesa	Y lo engatusé a cabriolas
Dejan entre otros horrores;	. . . .
Y no entienden los clamores	Hasta que al fin de un bolazo
Porque ciegos atropellan.	Del caballo lo bajé.
—*Santos Vega*, 62–63	—*Ida*, III

The Fight with the Gendarmes

ASCASUBI	HERNÁNDEZ
. . . y le soltó	Tuitos se me venían
Las bolas con tal certeza,	Donde yo los esperaba,
Que al tiro se las ató	. . . .
En las manos al rocín,	Pegué un brinco y entre todos
De suerte que allí rodó,	Sin miedo me entreveré
Y al gaucho haciendo cabriolas	. . . .
Por las orejas lo echó.	El más engolosinao
De parao salió el malevo,	Se me apió con un achazo
Como que era parador,	. . . .

Y creyendo resistirse
A su pistola acudió;
Pero al dir a martillarla,
Ahí mesmo se le cayó
El pie de gato del arma;
Y entonces quiso el facón
Pelar de entre las coronas
Pero tiempo no le dió
Genaro que se le vino
Listo encima, y le abocó
El naranjero, y le dijo:
¡Echate al suelo, ladrón!
Boca abajo; echate ya,
Ligero, porque si no,
Ni para enfermo te dejo
De un trabucazo. . . ¡Por Dios!

—*Ibid.*, 122–123

Antes de que diera un paso
Le eché tierra en los dos ojos
. . . .
Sentí que por las costillas
Un sable me hacía cosquillas—
. . . .
Dí para atrás unos pasos
Hasta que pude hacer pié,
Por delante me lo eché
De punta y tajos a un criollo;
Metió la pata en un oyo
Y yo al oyo lo mandé.
. . . .
Uno despachó al infierno
De dos que lo atropellaron,
Los demás remoliniaron,
Pues íbamos a la fija,
Y a poco andar dispararon
Lo mesmo que sabandija.

—*Ida*, IX

Ascasubi does not describe a fight as successfully as he depicts nature. Hernández, on the contrary, may be charged, in his descriptions of conflicts, with being bloody and barbarous, but he is at home in his battle scenes, and he certainly carries us with him! But of course fights are only one feature of gaucho narrations. Ascasubi may excel in descriptions of nature, but Hernández makes up for this in his character-sketches and social analyses. His men and women are not wishy-washy, but vital, burning lovers and haters. I say this especially of his men, for there are no extensive delineations of feminine character; nevertheless, the details concerning representatives of the fair sex are very just. Without doubt, whatever depth the personages of Hernández possess, is due in considerable degree to his lyric intensity. In this he shines by contrast with Ascasubi.

To conclude: Ascasubi is excellent in description and bizarre in phraseology. He can be satiric, dramatic, romantic, but he cannot—in *Santos Vega*—succeed in being lyric. Hernández never obtained from him, either by inspiration or by remote transmission, certain highly important factors which characterize *Martín Fierro*. These are: first, the epic feature of an archetype, struggling against an entirely hostile enviroment; second, the epic relations within the central theme; third, the unity consequent upon the introduction of only one hero; fourth, the amazing concreteness and swiftness with which large expanses of time and space are treated, and the rapidity in general—which is not to be accounted unworthy of Homer; fifth, the fecundity of comparisons; sixth, the depth of suffering and delicacy of feeling which transform the experience of one humble gaucho into something abiding and universal.

III

A Survey of Argentine Gaucho Literature

(*Continued*)

Contemporaries and Successors to José Hernández

THE WORKS OF ESTANISLAO DEL Campo (b. in Buenos Aires 1834, d. there, 1880), a faithful imitator of Ascasubi, are practically valueless—with the one striking exception of his *Fausto* (1870). Since this latter is noteworthy, and since del Campo is the only outstanding contemporary of Hernández who wrote gaucho poetry, we resume our survey appropriately with a brief discussion of this work, and a statement of what del Campo did for the author of *Martín Fierro*.

In this poem, which is written in the gaucho vernacular, the character, "Anastasio el Pollo," relates his impressions on hearing the opera *Faust* sung in the old Colón Theatre in Buenos Aires. The poem has some admirable lines, so admirable that they extort praise from Menéndez y Pelayo.[1]

Now whereas Ascasubi and Hernández succeeded, sometimes at least, in infusing into their poems an atmosphere of the nameless popular bards, not so much can be said of del Campo. The *Fausto* is a *tour de force:* its author was not a gaucho, but a city man of surprising versatility. You may strongly suspect that as he penned his *Fausto* his tongue was in his cheek. "See what I can do," you may imagine him saying, with a triumphant smile, to his brother-in-law, Ricardo Gutiérrez. "In what respects are Hidalgo and Ascasubi superior to me?"[2] It is well to lay stress on this attitude. That Ascasubi, del Campo, and Hernández should be grouped together, because of their eminence in gaucho literature, is natural. But the student must be put on his guard against taking for granted that del Campo's poem is a genuine, spontaneous gaucho song. Probably in Argentina, where it is much

---

1. *Op. cit.,* 472.
2. For an account of the inception of the *Fausto,* see Rojas, *Op. cit.,* 452.

admired,[3] very few are misled by its apparently genuine style; we of the North might well be, without some such word of caution.

But the *Fausto,* though a work of literary artifice, really has many fine poetic touches, many brief lines which convey abiding truths. The commendatory words of Menéndez y Pelayo, "this is good, wholesome, legitimate poetry," are not to be wondered at. The more I study the *Fausto,* the more I am convinced that a number of these worthy passages must have influenced José Hernández in the composition of *Martín Fierro.* I will briefly build up the case, by parallelisms as before, and leave the reader to judge of its plausibility.

Laguna says, in *Fausto:*[4]	Compare what Picardía says:
Y ¿sabe lo que decía	Lo hubieran visto afligido
Cuando se vía en la mala?	Llorar por las chucherías
El que me ha pelao la chala	"Ma gañao con picardía"
Debe tener brujería.	Decia el gringo y lagrimiaba,
—*Fausto,* I	Mientras yo en un poncho alzaba
	Todita su merchería.
	—*Vu,* XIII

What makes this parallel the more striking, is that not merely is the essential thought the same, but the very same rhymes are used: *-ía* and *a–a.*

Lest this should seem too far-fetched, I submit others.[5]

---

3. Cf. García Velloso: *Op. cit.,* 298 ff.

4.   Laguna:

   And you know what he said
   When he saw his luck was bad?
   "He who peeled my ear of maize
   Must know witchcraft."

   Picardía:

   You should have seen his affliction,
   How he wept for his trifles:
   "He win from me by de cheat"
   Kept saying this gringo, 'mid sobs,
   While in a poncho I was moving
   Away all his loved stock-in-trade.

5.   DEL CAMPO

   Some gringo, quick as light
   Working his fingers, it must have been,
   . . . To think I did not feel him!
   Anyhow, I crossed myself, to ward off his spells.
   There is no sorrow
   Like an unfortunate love.

     HERNÁNDEZ

   And never do they (i.e., the gringos) hesitate
   To "lift" others' possessions.

   From that day on,
   I knew all women, knowing one.

DEL CAMPO	HERNÁNDEZ
Algun gringo como luz	Y nunca se andan con chicas
Para la uña, ha de haber sido.	Para alzar ponchos ajenos.
—¡Y no haberlo yo sentido!	
En fin, yo le hice la cruz.	
—Fausto, II	*—Ida,* V
No hay desgracia ninguna	Las mujeres, desde entonces,
Como un desdichado amor.	Conocí a todas en una—
—Puede ser; pero, amigaso,	. . . .
Yo en las cuartas no me enredo	Mujer y perra parida,
. . . .	No se me atraca ninguna!
Por hembras yo no me pierdo.	
—Fausto, IV	*—Ida,* X
Ningun temor en el seno	Ah! pobre! si el mismo creiba,
De la pobrecita cabe,	Que la vida le sobraba,
Pues que se hamaca, no sabe,	Ninguno diría que andaba
Entre el fuego y el veneno.	Aguaitándolo la muerte.
—Fausto, VI	*—Ida,* VIII

The immediately preceding passages refer to persons so utterly unlike, that objection may be raised to including the lines as evidence. At least this cannot be denied, that the gaucho mind revelled in fatalistic phrases, whether applied to the tragedy of Gretchen, or the case of a border ruffian.

Now, leaving all the other, far more pleasing nature-studies which one finds in del Campo, let us compare this bit of romantic musing, in its natural setting, with similar lines offered by Hernández:[6]

—Maybe so, but, old man,	. . . .
I don't get mixed up in all that.	"Woman and bitch with pups"—
. . . .	None of that gets next to me.
I don't ruin myself for women.	
	Ah! luckless man! if he himself thought
No fear is in the breast	That life already was more than past,
Of that ill-fated girl.	None would have said that death
How can she know she's wav'ring now	Was camping on his trail.
Twixt fire and poison?	

6.
DEL CAMPO	HERNÁNDEZ
When all the world lies sleeping,	By some brookside
You, on your saddle-pillow	I would stay, solitary,
Wide-awake, toss and turn,	Meditating a thousand matters
Thinking of your deep affection.	And at some sudden turn,

Del Campo	Hernández
Cuando duerme todo el mundo,	En la orilla de un arroyo
Usté, sobre su recao,	Solitario lo pasaba,
Se da güeltas, desvelao,	En mis cosas cavilaba
Pensando en su amor projundo,	Y a una güelta repentina
	Se me hacía ver a mi china
Y si el viento hace sonar	O escuchar que me llamaba.
Su pobre techo de paja,	. . . .
Cree usté que es *ella* que baja	Pasa uno hasta sin comer
Sus lágrimas a secar.	Por pensar en su mujer,
	En sus hijos y en su pago.
Y si en alguna lomada	—*Vu,* II
Tiene que dormir al raso,	
Pensando en *ella,* amigaso,	
Lo hallará la madrugada.	
—*Fausto,* IV	

I am very far from saying that Hernández stole del Campo's thunder. The experiences we have discussed in this chapter were commonplaces, and Hernández knew them better even than del Campo.

Is it not remarkable, that in those last lines from *Martín Fierro,* there is not only the same general idea as in del Campo's *cuartetas,* but also practically the same specific image of the agency that causes the lover to fancy the loved one present? Del Campo makes the agency wind in the thatch; Hernández cannot resort to this device, for the lover is out of doors. Therefore, he employs those glints of sunshine, fleeting shadows, and quick-dying breezes which often half-persuade us of a presence. . .

I am inclined to think that here Hernández is following quite closely a suggestion from del Campo. If so, no guilt attaches to the deed. He is

---

And if the wind whispers
Through your humble roof of thatch,

You think it's she who's coming down
To dry your tears.

And if, on some hill.
You must sleep out all night,
Thinking of her, old man,
Dawn will come upon you.

I'd fancy I saw my wife
Or heard her calling me.
. . . .
One even goes dinnerless.
Thinking of his wife,
Of his children, of his country.

paying tribute to an excellent poet, in whom he has discovered the same worth that Menéndez y Pelayo praises.[7] Hernández was criticised severely on the publication of Part I of *Martín Fierro*: perhaps some admittedly popular verses of Part II are a sop thrown to the critics. And the charming lyric passages in del Campo might well stir any man to emulation.

What cannot be asserted is that Hernández borrowed the element of *compañerismo* (friendship) from del Campo's very loving pair of gauchos. We have seen the two gauchos in *Santos Vega* and in Hidalgo. We have seen how the *cielo* introduces couples to sing, as well as dance. The reader will have already recalled instances of companionship in the popular literature of many other lands.

Whatever historical interest, whatever uniqueness of presentation, whatever literary value may have been accredited to the forms we have thus far considered, these qualities will be found to belong supremely to the *Martín Fierro* of José Hernández. The more one studies the whole range of gaucho literature, the more one is convinced that it was necessary for a line of gaucho poets to *lead up* to Hernández, affording him a proper background, while others in the line were similarly destined to follow him. *Martín Fierro*, since its publication in 1872 and 1878, has held the center of the stage.

After its appearance, no other lyrico-epic poet arose to give us, *in gaucho speech*, the gaucho's story. Nor was this necessary, for any gaps in the cycle of *Santos Vega*, *Fausto*, and *Martín Fierro* are amply supplied by the poems of Hidalgo, Mitre, Echeverría, and others. But Martín Fierro's influence has only just begun. His line has not yet gone out through all the earth, and yet his impress is to be seen in all the literary forms we shall now proceed briefly to consider; and this impress is one of the most eloquent testimonies to the immediate triumph of the poem, to the respect and consideration at once accorded it as a literary force and factor.

The facts concerning *Martín Fierro*, its origin, publication, reception, the exposition of its story, the commentary on gaucho and Indian life, and the attempt to evaluate the poem as literature, are all to be presented hereafter. This immediate survey undertakes only to demonstrate how these two contemporaries, del Campo and Hernández, the last great gaucho writers—and supremely Hernández—took up gratefully the

---

7. Did I not fear to be accused of over-ingenuity, I should hint at the possibility of another imitation in the negro's song about the sea in *Vu*, XXX.

torch their forerunners laid down, and how Hernández passed on a shining light to his successors.

Just as Hidalgo had decidedly influenced Hernández in both subject-matter and form, just as del Campo had influenced him in form, so Hernández exercised an influence over Florencio Iriarte, whose *Rosendo Flores* fills twenty-three closely printed pages in Maucci's *Parnaso Argentino* (second edition).

The plot of this recital is commonplace enough: two young gauchos, both crossed in love, and cursing everything, including their own existence, meet, and in the bond of misery swear an oath of brotherhood. Shortly afterward, they participate in an Indian fight, and one of them, Contreras, is mortally wounded. His comrade takes him to the nearest rancho. The woman who helps to lay Contreras upon his deathbed is discovered to be his old flame. The shock of his death proves too much for her. She falls dying, but only after having laid in his fellow gaucho's arms the babe she bore to Contreras' rival.

Compare the following lines in the two poems respectively:[8]

Rosendo Flores[9]	*Martín Fierro*
Aquí me pongo a cantar.	Aquí me pongo a cantar.
—p. 434	—*Ida*, I
Lo hice cantar pal carnero.	Y ya cantó pa el carnero.
—p. 450	—*Ida*, VII
Y del flete lo bajé.	Del caballo lo bajé.
—p. 452	—*Ida*, III
Gargantiando como zapos.	Como la garganta al sapo.
—p. 452	—*Ida*, III

---

8. For the citations from *Rosendo Flores* I have employed the edition referred to above.

9.

Rosendo Flores	*Martín Fierro*
Here I start to sing.	Here I start to sing.
I made him sing for the burying-ground.	And already he sang for the burying-ground.
And I downed him from his steed.	From the horse I downed him.
Croaking like frogs.	Like a frog's throat.
And in that tanned countenance Two tears gathered.	And two big tears rolled down Fierro's cheek.

Y en aquel rostro tostado
Dos lágrimas se cuajaron.
—p. 454

Y a Fierro dos lagrimones
Le rodaron por la cara.
—*Ida*, XIII

These few striking resemblances culled among the many, simply prove that the popular phrases have been given their "hallmark" in the poem of *Martín Fierro*. Henceforth, no writer who aims at producing a true gaucho poem can risk taking a different model.

Note, too, before we leave this tale of Flores, that he found an *aparcero*, as Martín found Cruz; and compare the pitiful deaths of both these *aparceros*.

Rafael Obligado (1851–1920) is not so much a gaucho as was Hernández, but he is permeated by the gaucho tradition—he loves the gaucho atmosphere—he venerates the legendary gaucho minstrels. Undoubtedly he was under the spell of Hernández. The sympathy breathing through his *Santos Vega* (1885), *La prenda del payador* (1885), *El himno de Santos Vega* (1906), and *La muerte del payador* (1885), is too great, too genuine for him not to recognize the primacy of Hernández. Of Santos Vega, we have already heard. Mitre fostered the legend that had been growing up about the picturesque personality of this arch-troubadour; Ascasubi lent it all the influence of his facile pen; many a lesser poet incorporated the theme in his lyrics; Hernández showed what were the flesh-and-blood qualities of another such *payador;* and finally, Obligado made a lasting place in Argentine literature for the well-loved Vega, who, after years of supremacy in song, was vanquished at last in a contest of minstrelsy and died brokenhearted in consequence. Folk-lore has it that his antagonist was none other than the devil!

The myth of Santos Vega could not exist in a land where *Martín Fierro* would be unwelcome. Martín, though a successor of the great Santos, has helped by his popularity to pave the way for that greater glory which Vega now enjoys. The whole subject of the myth of Santos Vega, to which fuller attention cannot be given here, has been studied with genuine scholarly zeal by Roberto Lehmann-Nitsche.[10]

I mention Ricardo Gutiérrez (*Lázaro, La Fibra Salvaje*) only as fresh evidence of the hold which, after the publication of *Martín Fierro*, the gaucho tradition took upon all literary Argentina. Gutiérrez' poems are not "popular," either in origin or appeal. The style is "cultured," with

---

10. *Santos Vega*, in the *Boletín de la Academia Nacional de Ciencias*, Vol. XXII, 1917.

frequent attempts at the grandiose—attempts not always successful. The general effect is a tone of melancholy, reminding us at times of Espronceda; the style is often turgid, bombastic, unreal. We must not, however, deny the existence of real feeling in *Lázaro* and *La Fibra Salvaje*.

Among shorter poems, Belisario Roldán's *Ante-Raza* in *Bajo la toca de lino* excels. The verses are polished and pleasing, and the theme of the bygone gaucho generations, their descent, physically and spiritually, from those stern warriors who hurled back the Crescent in Spain—task of seven hundred years!—is treated with sympathy, persuasiveness, and deep feeling. Nevertheless, this is not a popular work. We stand off and look at the gaucho. The sight is interesting, but we do not get to the depths of his heart. It is worth our while, however, to study a poem like *Ante-Raza* and then read again *Martín Fierro*. We shall see the more clearly, how Hernández, though giving to his poem an unmistakeable parentage, really accomplished wonders in approximating the spirit, and, in numerous passages, the style, of the popular anonymous poetry of Argentina.

As might be expected, all epic qualities vanish sooner or later from the latest phase of gaucho poetry. It becomes pure lyric. Some of the songs sung in Argentina—of the *ombú*, of the Dulcineas, of pampa hardships, are truly moving. Excellent examples are found in Martiniano Leguizamón's *Calandria*[11] and Javier de Viana's *Gaucha*.[12] The study of Lehmann-Nitsche: *Santos Vega*,[13] may also be consulted.

The *payada de contrapunto* or match of two "guitarrists" in lyrical improvisation in *Martín Fierro*, has made similar manifestations almost as fashionable in latter-day literature as they were among the gauchos sung by Hernández. One of the best-known literary examples of the *contrapunto* was published in a "comic" weekly in Buenos Aires some years ago. It is satiric, and represents Sr. Quintana, at one time president of Argentina, in animated conversation with Sr. Avellaneda, another prominent political personage. Another *payada* takes place in *Santos Vega*, a novel by Eduardo Gutiérrez, who is discussed in the following pages.

What connection has all this with *Martín Fierro?* The answer is easy. The mantle of Fierro has fallen on these moderns. Such contests as the

---

11. 131–2, 157–168.

12. *Passim.*

13. 305–318 *et passim.*

payadas occurred up to within very recent years in both the large Plata cities, and were duly chronicled in the press. Probably the custom still survives in some obscure provincial nooks. Such writers as have been named, and a host of others, have furnished part of the mental pabulum of the country for years. And as I read them, or read about them, I see that *Martín Fierro* is always present, more or less consciously, as the basis of comparison.

To illustrate. A certain poet, praising the manly beauty of *Santos Vega*, writes:[14]

> *And you would say of Vega and Fierro*
> *That they are brothers of the same race.*

César Hidalgo says:[15]

> *The ombú keeps in its leaves*
> *The accent of Martín Fierro*
> *And the pure feeling*
> *That he poured out in his song.*

A great newspaper, *El Día* of Montevideo, says the following of a *payador*, May 26, 1892: "When we hear him, we think of the lines of Hernández, that verses gush from his lips like streams from a spring."[16]

Imonti in *Bordoneos* tells us that[17]

> *One hears the melancholy accents*
> *Of Hernández and Santos Vega,*
> *Like lost laments*
> *Borne to our ears.*

Miguel de Unamuno, the eminent Spanish writer, said:[18] "Were I to go now to Argentina, I should find that more than *one* peasant, instead of talking the picturesque language of Santos Vega or Martín Fierro, would speak to me in Sicilian or in the Basque tongue."

---

14. Lehmann-Nitsche, *Santos Vega*, 295.

15. *Ibid.*, 296–7.

16. *Ida*, I.

17. *Pampa Argentina*, July 17, 1910.

18. *La Ilustración española y americana*, July 22, 1899.

Here, then, is the conclusion. Just as we call English the language of Shakespeare and Milton, identifying the language by naming its chief poets, so when we speak of gaucho poetry, we say it is the speech that bears the impress of José Hernández and his *Martín Fierro*.

In the novel, the gaucho type was fixed by Eduardo Gutiérrez (1853–1890). More than his so-called historical novels, such as *La Mazorca* and *El puñal del Tirano*, his "bandit tales," especially *Juan Moreira* and *Santos Vega*, have a permanent appeal.

Moreira was a notorious outlaw in Buenos Aires Province during the sixties, and Gutiérrez wrote up his adventures in just such a superficial, episodic manner as would please his daily newspaper *clientèle*. In the novel Moreira won the hearts of the masses. Its thesis is somewhat similar to that of *Martín Fierro*. A decent gaucho, too long outraged by more powerful neighbors, takes a dramatic revenge, then turns outlaw and lives in constant conflict with organized authority until the day of his violent death.

In *Santos Vega* and *Una amistad hasta la muerte,* which are but the two parts of a connected narrative, the *Fierro* influence is very marked. The plot of the novel is related at great length in Lehmann-Nitsche.[19] Aside from the prominence given to the various loves by which Santos is swayed, the intrigue is so akin to that of *Martín Fierro* that the reader might well be justified in thinking that he had found the "little brother" of our work. Vega is forced into the outlaw life; he "kills his man," now at a ball in a private house, now in a *pulpería;* he engages in a wonderful *payada de contrapunto* with a negro and thoroughly vanquishes him; he has a faithful friend Carmona, whose death he laments as Martín grieves over that of Cruz; he is a prisoner among the Indians for two years; and on his return he weeps over the past, like Martín. To this day, the "good outlaw," romantic, melancholy, excellent guitarrist and singer, with his superb horse and the trusty weapons which wellnigh invariably turn to flight his pursuers, is the popular literary hero in Argentina. And yet, though Gutiérrez won all hearts, who would exchange the art of *Martín Fierro* for the sensationalism of Gutiérrez' *Santos Vega?* The superiority of Hernández—always assuming that one may reasonably compare a prose work with a poetical production treating the same theme—is evident on making the most casual examination of the respective *payadas*. Gutiérrez stimulates and gratifies our love for

---

19. *Op. cit.,* 133–156.

HENRY A. HOLMES AND JOSÉ HERNÁNDEZ

strong, crude effects; Hernández, on the other hand, deftly lures his willing Muse. In none of the later *payadas* is there combined such sober, elevated thought with lyricism so sure and beautiful.

To conclude, *Juan Moreira* and *Santos Vega* are not other *Martín Fierros* refurbished for the day's *feuilleton;* but they are infused with much of the same spirit. Eduardo Gutiérrez, though only nineteen years of age, was well started on his journalistic career when *Martín Fierro* saw the light. *Juan Moreira* and *Santos Vega* appear as newspaper serials in 1880, the former being finished in March of 1881, and the later running in *La Patria Argentina* from November until May of that year. Public appreciation of *Martín Fierro* was at a height, which made it impossible for the fluent pen of Gutiérrez not to treat the same subject, the same scenes, the same details. His most striking divergencies from Hernández' methods are the use of prose, the accumulation of disconnected and wildly improbable incidents (whereas Hernández strung his cantos on a real if slender thread of plot), the manner of death of his heroes, and the imparting of a certain professional air to all their exploits, quite foreign to *Martín Fierro*. Gutiérrez was a careless journalist, not an artist.

Other novelists who have kept the gaucho fire burning are Leguizamón, whose *Montaraz* has certain noble touches that remind us of the *Facundo* of Sarmiento; Javier de Viana, a literary portraitist of more than average ability—however he is an Uruguayan; Daireaux, Cambaceres, Regules, Ugarte, Bunge, Payró—but let us not extend the list.

We have seen that after the *gesta* of Hernández, came the scattered songs, the lyrics; then the chronicle; lastly, came the drama. *Martín Fierro*, potentially, has all the dramatic elements. Once this lyric passion cools, and can be made to serve—once this rapid, sweeping action is held in "situations"—you have only to ring up the curtain. This was done with huge success by the Podestá dramatic company, in March and April, 1890. Here was the second gaucho drama. Podestá had represented *Juan Moreira*, the first, in 1884 and 1886. *Martín Fierro* was first put on the boards in La Plata. It had been dramatized by Elias Regules.[20]

The Podestás were followed in gaucho plays by Camila Quiroga and her company, and a host of others. Moreira almost elbowed Fierro off

---

20. Lehmann-Nitsche, *Op. cit.*, 217, 218.

the stage. *Santos Vega*, dramatized by Nosiglia and others, has become a common theatrical *bonne bouche*.

A partial list of the earlier native dramas is given in Lehmann-Nitsche. To anyone wishing to study the Argentine stage, may be recommended especially the critical comment evoked by the première of *Calandria* in 1896.[21]

Later, Florencio Sánchez (Uruguayan) captivated South American and also Spanish audiences, with his extension of the problem of Hernández. The gaucho father comes into conflict with his citified son in that charming bit of stage-craft, *M'Hijo el Dotor*. It is merely Sánchez' artistic mode of saying that the new days and the new ways are forcing the gaucho to the wall. Naturally, he lacks the desert, the savages, the wild impressiveness of *Martín Fierro*.

The latest invasion of *Martín Fierro's* domain is by "movie writers." And the most faithful presentment of the gauchos on the screen, if one is to "follow the crowd," is found in *Nobleza Gaucha*, which has been known to River Plate audiences for at least seven years. Many of the features are Fierroesque, but the makers of the film drama saw to it that *Nobleza Gaucha* should not lack what *Martín Fierro* lacks so palpably—a heroine.

I have not had the good fortune to see *Martín Fierro* in a moving picture, but a "colossal" success might be predicted, out-of-hand, for such a representation. Of course it would abound in *escenas campestres* ("camp scenes", in Anglo-Argentine argot): the corral, the *tranquera* (gate), the low *rancho* with thatched roof, the *pulpería*, inevitable store-saloon, the ombú-tree, the out-door fires, round which sit the gauchos sipping Paraguayan *mate*, the *china* (wife) of Fierro, with bright-colored dress and gracefully knotted kerchief, the guitars, the songs and dances, the love scenes and the fights—these, and far more than these, would thrill a spectator to laughter or tears.

All the above is, of course, little more than a catalogue, with some hints of criticism. The attempt to realize in what respects, and how deeply, José Hernández' work has impressed itself upon the popular consciousness, is made elsewhere in this study, in the conviction that life, and tributes to life, can not be adequately interpreted by dates or lists of names.

---

21. Reviews, etc., in *La Nación, El Tiempo*, and *La Tribuna*, May, 1896.

IV

The Life and Writings of Hernández

José Hernández was born in the *partido* of San Martín, in the Province of Buenos Aires, November 10, 1834. The *partido* may be compared to our township. That of San Martín is near the metropolis. Nowadays, electric cars make communication between city and suburb an affair of half an hour. This was not the case in the time of Hernández. I imagine him racing his pony over the broad fields that are now the army training-ground. I see him reining up beside the old well, where even today the patient horses walk their interminable round, to draw up water for the fields. Or at dusk I see him moving toward the family mansion, past the rank hedges and aromatic trees of paradise. San Martín today is a delight, especially in the luxuriant Argentine spring time: one is glad to believe that in Hernández' youth it was not less so.

Here were spent his most impressionable years. And let it not be thought that he grew up in an ordinary family circle. On the maternal side, the family was "patrician," and related to that of Pueyrredón, then and now an honored line. "And it is not inopportune to note that Doña Juana Manuela Gorriti, daughter of a hero of the struggle for independence, calls José Hernández 'My dear Cousin,' so that the author of *Martín Fierro* was connected by blood with some of the families who achieved our emancipation."[1] "José lived," says Bunge's edition of *Martín Fierro*,[2] "the customs that he was later to reflect in his celebrated work." And as the years passed, he was sent by his parents, for the sake of his health, to certain *estancias* in the South, where, close to the frontier, he learned what Indians were like and even took a young man's part in the desperate warfare between gauchos and savages. Details of his education are lacking. That, formally or otherwise, he made the acquaintance of "the rhetoricians," is plain from his long journalistic and literary activity. That he had "specialized" may be inferred from the fact that he was stenographer for the Senate of the Confederation, in Entre Ríos, in those years between the downfall of Rosas and the

---

1. Rojas, *Op. cit.,* 464–5.
2. Published by *La Cultura Argentina*: Biographical Preface.

battle of Pavón (1852–1861). During this period, he also shared in the military campaigns, on the Urquiza side, and rose to the grade of sergeant major.[3] He was second in charge of the National Audit Bureau. He was also private secretary for a time to Governor Pedernera of Entre Ríos. But of course the Confederation went to pieces after Pavón. Mitre and his Buenos Aires partisans came uppermost, and Mitre was elected president. Hernández seems to have been a consistent political opponent of Mitre for many years—at any rate, he so writes when he sends Mitre a complimentary copy of *Martín Fierro,* of the edition of 1878. A facsimile of this letter is reproduced in the introduction to the edition of *La Biblioteca Argentina.*

The defeat of the federated elements did not make the "airs" of Buenos Aires any more enticing to José Hernández than they had been since Alsina and his fellow "Unitarians" returned from the exile into which Rosas had forced them. Accordingly he continues his provincial existence, publishes a *Life of the Chacho* (the Chacho, like Rosas, was a leader of the gauchos), and we next see him designated *fiscal* and secretary of the treasury for Corrientes Province. Having resided in the river provinces, it was natural that he should engage in the clashes between the Buenos Aires forces and the *Correntinos* and *Entrerrianos* led by López Jordán, 1870–1872. Two distinct uprisings failed, and López Jordán was at last (1872) driven over the border into Brazil. Hernández followed him loyally—some say on foot. (He was very stout.) He had been zealous in conspiring against Sarmiento's government, establishing himself in a Buenos Aires hostel in 1872, and soliciting men and money for the rebellion. We shall revert presently to this episode. Such periods of exile as that of Hernández are not always lengthy, and after an interval passed in Montevideo, we see him in the Argentine once more (ca. 1874).

López Jordán's uprising was the last of the gaucho insurrections. In his natal province, Hernández lived, for a goodly number of years, the life of a legislator and administrator and greatly esteemed citizen. After 1880, Buenos Aires Province had to create for itself a separate capital, as the Federal government took over the metropolis for the Federal capital. It was the provincial governor, Dardo Rocha, who conceived the plan of building an up-to-date seat of provincial administration, and today the handsome city of La Plata is a monument to him and

---

3. Cf. Rojas, *Op. cit.,* 467.

men like Hernández, who in the current press and in the provincial legislature advocated Rocha's measures. As a provincial deputy, he frequently, while chatting with his friends, referred to the subject of his debates, saying that he owed his measure of success to his earlier experiences as stenographer at Paraná.[4] Some of his fellow-legislators were men of prominence, but among them he held his own. In politics, he opposed not only Mitre but also Sarmiento, the two Argentines whom we regard, perhaps, with the greatest veneration. But some of the planks of their platform were proved impossible, a result which Hernández had foreseen. We are told that when he made his political addresses, his voice, powerful as the rolling swells of an organ, sent his friends into ecstasies. It is not difficult to understand, in view of these successes, why Hernández also held directorships in the National Bank of Mortgages and in the Council of Education.

The progressive governor, Rocha, wished to send him to Australia on a mission relating to the farming and stock-raising in which he was so well versed. Hernández declined, but wrote a valuable treatise, *Instrucción del estanciero*, which is still in vogue.

His journalistic labors are notable. In the late sixties, he was editing in Buenos Aires the *Revista del Río de la Plata*, a partisan (federal) sheet, whose policy advocated "Election of municipal officials; abolition of forcible raising of troops for frontier service; election of justices of the peace, of commandants, and of school boards."

It is interesting to read as a sample of the amenities of public life, the following reference to him by General Mansilla in his *Excursión a los Indios Ranqueles*,[5] which first appeared at this time: . . . "Our colleague Hernández, ex-editor of the *Río de la Plata*, whose bulging obesity is assuming more and more alarming proportions to those who are fond of him, as I am; for his girth threatens to swell until it reaches the regions of ether, or bursts like a Paraguayan torpedo." Besides the *Río de la Plata*, Bunge[6] cites other federal organs which he guided at other periods: *El Argentino* in Entre Ríos and *La Patria* in Montevideo—this latter a memorial to his days of exile within the period 1872–1874.

Of course the reader is curious to know if he wrote other poems besides *Martín Fierro*, and the reply, unfortunately, must be in the

---

4. Rojas, *Op. cit.*, 468.

5. 197.

6. *Op. cit.*, *loc. cit.*

affirmative. The 1894 edition of *Martín Fierro* includes the wholly uninspired short pieces: *El Viejo y la Niña, Los Dos Besos, El Carpintero,* and *Cantares.*

Probably there are at least a few others, but happily they remain in deepest obscurity. *Verbum sap!*

Hernández died in Belgrano, a fashionable quarter of Buenos Aires, October 10, 1894.

He had long been a striking figure on the streets of the capital, which was not then, as it now is, a world city. His luxuriant, Jove-like beard, immense frame, and benign countenance were imposing, while certain details of his costume, such as the gaucho hat and sometimes the top boots, were in no wise ridiculous. Such was the man, sincere, friendly, impressionable, *noblote.*[7] Calixto Oyuela, who must have known him well and long, told the present writer that he considered *Martín Fierro* artistic in the sense that its author moulded and massed and otherwise disposed his material to suit his literary purpose. He had led the gaucho life, but as an artist he was able to see it apart from himself and make it serve him. I did not understand Dr. Oyuela to discredit at all the genuineness of the gaucho days of Hernández, in spite of his high-born origin and subsequent prominent career.

In discussing Hernández' protest against injustice done the gauchos, Rojas and other critics seem to have overlooked an intensely human and thrillingly epic detail, and this I should like to comment upon here. In a later chapter I shall consider the epic value of the "struggle against civilization," which I shall endeavor to show was not the sole influence controlling the production of *Martín Fierro.*

What was the origin of Hernández' great poem? As we have seen, he was working for the López Jordán movement. His heart was full of resentment against practices oppressive to the gaucho, and he might have arraigned such oppression, using due caution, in various public ways. But according to unwritten law, the gauchos had been outraged in their most sacred, primitive rights, and their natural recourse was the appeal to arms. Such a resort did not seem less natural to Hernández, nor indeed would it so have seemed to Mitre. The latter's life was one long succession of uprisings against those he considered to be wrongfully in power. Thus it was the lust of battle, not the complacent smirk of the pamphleteer or the mere rhymer, that shone in the eyes of our poet. He

---

7. Rojas, *Op. cit.,* 464.

was already savoring the stern joy of the tremendous gallops which he sings; of the soldier's hazardous life; of scanty meals hastily cooked by the bivouac fire; of pursuit and condign punishment; and—sweetest of all—of resounding blows struck at city scoundrels in frock-coats. Ho! for camp and open plain, for *bolas* and lasso and careering steed! Our instinct assures us that Don José felt the divine afflatus. Enthusiasm possessed him. His blood coursed with epic swiftness. He no longer regarded the gaucho merely as one of the elements in the national make-up: he *felt* him to the depths of his own individual being; nay, he himself *was* the gaucho, eager to submit all to the supreme arbitrament of war.

But the hotel-corridors where Hernández hobnobbed with fellow-conspirators furnished no adequate initial impulse to the singer thrilling with his as yet wordless song. Let us change the figure: the machine is charged: it only awaits a spark. Who will supply it? Lugones in *El Payador*[8] finds a motive for the appearance of *Martín Fierro* in the publication, in Buenos Aires, of *Los Tres Gauchos Orientales y el Matrero Luciano Santos* by Antonio Lussich, June 14, 1872. This work abounded in Uruguayan revolutionary scenes. Hernández sent Lussich his thanks on June 20, and in December *Martín Fierro* was given to the public. Now, whoever reads Lugones, fascinating as his work is, will observe that he gives no thought to the surging, anticipatory emotion of Hernández, which meant power, nor yet sufficient consideration to the work of Lussich as an artistically prepared suggestion. Lugones speaks of it as an opportune stimulus, and says that Hernández, receiving it, had "the happy thought" of writing *Martín Fierro.*

But he does not see that what Hernández needed was guidance, not prodding—favorable circumstances, the contagion of composition in the gaucho genre. The Muses saw to it that apology and polemic were for the nonce moved "up stage." Lussich suggests the form, octosyllabics—if indeed such suggestion was necessary. He also suggests (oh, it is the merest hint of a suggestion, if you like) the type of the gaucho hero: the *matrero* or outlaw. Otherwise we might have Hernández trying to produce an epic without a hero. So by one of those felicitous convergences which abound in literary history, a gaucho rebellion furnished the combustibles and Lussich may be said to have provided the spark. How bright was that spark, is apparent by the contrasted dimness of portions of *La Vuelta.*

---

8. 188–189.

But, says someone, the author's prefatory letter to his publisher, Don José Zoilo Miguens, seems to be convoying an apologetic work. Perhaps, in view of political conditions, a smoke-screen was advisable. Whatever the preface, in *La Ida* we have no apology. It is the *gesta* par excellence of the gauchos. The hero, Fierro, is a *cantor* in the gaucho sense,[9] which means that he has a genius for improvising verses which he sings to his guitar. It means, also, that in epic fashion, he recks nothing of precise details. He speaks in the first person, then suddenly dramatizes as Cruz comes upon the stage, and refers to himself as "he." He can never be consoled for the loss of his wife, yet he cheers Cruz with the remark that "perhaps some Indian lass will take pity on us." Inconsistencies truly epic! But whoever has gazed at a glowing, raging fire, has seen that its tongues dart this way and that: they are not fused. Fierro may well be inspired, but he is not apologetic.

Hernández might be justly proud of the immediate and widespread demand for his work, once this was given to the public. It was of course only Part I of the entire work, to be universally known as *La Ida,* after the publication in 1878 of *La Vuelta de Martín Fierro.* The demand for the poem has never ceased. From 1872 to 1875, eight editions appeared in Buenos Aires, a ninth in Rosario. The edition of 1894 estimates a sale of 64,000 copies up to that date. Rojas[10] in 1917 gives a figure of 100,000 to that date. These figures, it is true, include the sales for six years, of the separately published Part I.[11] The editions have been as varied in appearance as they have been in the place of their publication. Lugones speaks of a *cuaderno,* i.e., a rough, paper-covered copy, in a rancho among the Cordoban hills, being guarded jealously by an aged couple, both illiterate. Typographical errors, infelicities, and orthographical inconsistencies, have apparently marked nearly all editions. That of 1894 is, I suppose, a marvel of accuracy and excellence

9. Cf. Coester, *Literary History of Spanish America*, 135.

10. *Op. cit.,* 471 N.

11. The latest editions of which I have cognizance are: that edited by Carlos O. Bunge, in the series of *La Cultura Argentina* and bearing the date 1919; that edited by Juan José de Soiza Reilly in the series of *El Libro Criollo,* bearing the date of 1920 and contining Part I only; and that published by *Nosotros,* a Buenos Aires magazine, and bearing the date of 1920. The editor is Folco Testena, an Italian author. He has arranged in parallel columns the gaucho verses and a poetical Italian translation. The preface and notes are sympathetic and sometimes illuminating.

in comparison with some of the "pirated" editions.[12] Nevertheless, this fifteenth edition (published by the *Librería Martín Fierro* of Buenos Aires) is adorned with "fearful and wonderful" cuts, has an editorial preface which is no model of pure grammar; exhibits wretched taste and unpardonable transpositions in the "appreciations" which precede the poem as well as in the actual text—but it is better to draw a decent veil over the involuntary tragedy!

With the *Martín Fierro* published in 1919 by the *Biblioteca Argentina* (Ricardo Rojas, editor), we come at last to a real attempt to clear the ground for later critical editions. I use this text of *Martín Fierro* as relatively definitive. Rojas justifies his choice of text in the Introduction.[13] Speaking of the copy sent by the poet himself to Mitre with a dedication in his own handwriting, he says: "The First Part, authenticated by the signature of the poet (i.e. in the dedication), and the Second Part by the corrections of Hernández, since this was the first edition of Part II, make the copy in the Mitre Museum a supreme authority." On this Museum copy, the text in Rojas' edition is based.

Praise, honors, recognition of all kinds came to our author, from every part of Spanish America, from Spain and even from New York and Paris. Two quotations may suffice to indicate how very general was the applause of Hernández' contemporaries. The first is from so eminent a litterateur as Ricardo Palma,[14] who says of Cantos XXX and XXXII of *La Vuelta:* "They are two pictures from the pen of a master. To dedicate yourself, as you do, to popular poetry, is to fulfil a holy office." Going to the other extreme, I take the second from a humble *pulpero,* keeper of a "country store," who sent the following order to his wholesale dealers in Buenos Aires:[15] "Send me. . . 12 gross of matches; one barrel of beer; . . . 12 *Vueltas de Martín Fierro;* 100 tins of sardines."

There were, and are still, dissenting voices, which will be noticed elsewhere.

Six years passed. As we have seen, the appeal to arms was getting more and more unfashionable as a political solution. José Hernández fought solely with his pen and his brain, after the defeat of López Jordán. But, absorbed as he was in public duties, his heart ached for his

---

12. The second-hand bookseller who sold me a copy congratulated me on making a bargain, since copies were becoming very rare.

13. xii–xiii.

14. Edition of 1894 of *Martín Fierro: Juicios Críticos* xii.

15. Rojas, *Op. cit.,* 472.

old gaucho acquaintances, who were not only tyrannized over by the military power, but also exploited by numerous civil elements; judges, gendarmes, merchants, political bosses, and ranchers. How speak a word for this oppressed and despairing class? For the hour of the last fatal retreat had come for the gauchos during Sarmiento's régime. As a national faction, as a quasi-independent, turbulent element, the gauchos were beginning to disappear. If it might be a wingéd word!

Was the *payador*, the gaucho troubadour, Fierro, vanished for aye beyond the western sky-line? Hernández evidently thought not. He proceeded, in the latter part of the year 1878, to bring back Fierro from his Indian asylum and put a new, very much longer narrative in his mouth. *Hinc illae lacrimae*, of Fierro for his comrade Cruz, of his sons, and of Picardía. In spite of obvious faults *La Vuelta de Martín Fierro* is a masterly exposition of gaucho life. It is also a serious indictment, a deliberate flagellation, of the abuses which broke up the homes of Fierro and Cruz. It was received with the same approval as *La Ida*. No one has ever heard the ruder elements, to whom it made a peculiar appeal, complain of its defects. And perhaps they seize upon its merits as the more literate cannot.

La Ida had contained 2310 lines, and now *La Vuelta* displayed 4893. It was published by Don José Puig y Clavero, who was as much amazed as the critics, over the success obtained. Perhaps Hernández was likewise surprised, but one doubts it. He had heard the hostile criticism referred to above, and he had tried to profit by it; but in his heart there was always a serene faith, which finds vivid expression in a couplet of Canto XXXIII, and which has been amply justified:[16]

> *Me tendrán en su memoria*
> *Para siempre, mis paisanos.*

16.
> *For ever in memory*
> *My fellow-countrymen will keep me.*

V

The Story of "Martín Fierro"

Travelers who have the good fortune to find themselves in Buenos Aires, feel after a few days an overmastering desire to see the Argentine pampa. From the capital these plains stretch away indefinitely, westward and southwestward and southward. To call them "vast," "interminable," is merely to provoke impatience among the initiated. But how difficult it is to find other adjectives as true and less trite, to describe the pampa! No trees? No. Except, perhaps, in several miles' expanse, one lonely *ombú,* and what a tree: gnarly of trunk, roaming of root, prodigal of shade! Its homely dignity accentuates the sublime solitude. In these days the whizzing train takes the traveler rapidly over such expanses, but whether they occur in the fertile Province of Buenos Aires, or westward in the arid mediterranean region, the landscape ensemble is one, not of barrenness, but of bareness. For there may be great fertility: rich pasturage, actual or potential, for millions of animals, yet with it the silence and loneliness of the desert! You advance a few miles on this imposing stage, and your eye lights on a herd of pampa horses or cattle. Thrilling sight! At a fresh undulation, you come upon, perhaps a ranch with extensive buildings, perhaps only a *rancherío* (humble dwelling of the peasant), perhaps only a *tapera* or abandoned pampa home. You may never be as far from all the results of advancing civilization as you think, but the unpeopled vastness will make you agree with this description in *Martín Fierro:*[1]

> *Todo es cielo y horizonte*
> *En inmenso campo verde!*
> *Pobre de aquel que se pierde*
> *O que su rumbo estravea!*
>
> . . . .
> *No hay auxilio que esperar,*

---

1. "All is sky and horizon on that immense green plain. Woe to him who loses his way! . . . With no hope of human aid, let him look solely to God. In the desert rarely does one escape."

Solo de Dios hay amparo—
En el desierto es muy raro
Que uno se pueda escapar.

—*Vu*, X

Such the stage of the pampa, whose "genius" is seen later in this work as providing the "antagonist" in our desert drama. We have already studied, slightly, the "chorus" of gauchos whose habitat is the pampa. The "hero" is Martín Fierro. The author himself, Hernández, keeps pretty much in the background, and puts the tale in Martín's mouth. The latter becomes the "protagonist," not for himself alone, but as representative of his class.

We assume the rôle of respectful listeners as Fierro tunes his guitar. He is no novice. Singer of stories is he, and more, for he composes his verses as he sings them—a *payador*.

"He recalls in a poetic contrast the days when he was a good father and loyal husband: distilling in impressive stanzas his experience of suffering, for (he says) 'nothing teaches us like suffering and tears.' He then descants on the days when the pampa was happy (think of them as in the earlier 'sixties of the nineteenth century)—until that golden age ceased. . . and the peace of the gaucho's fireside was succeeded by military persecution by levies, fraudulent elections, and frontier garrison duty, the period contemporary with gaucho decadence."[2]

1—
Aquí me pongo a cantar
Al compás de la vigüela,
Que el hombre que lo desvela
Una pena estrordinaria,
Como la ave solitaria
Con el cantar se consuela.

1—
Here I sit down to sing
To the rhythm of the guitar,
For he who is beset
By extraordinary anguish,
Like the lonely bird
Consoles himself with song.

2—
Pido a los Santos del Cielo
Que ayuden mi pensamiento,
Les pido en este momento

2—
I ask the saints above
To aid my thought,
I beg them at this moment

---

2. Rojas, *Op. cit.*, 483.

Que voy a contar mi historia
Me refresquen la memoria
Y aclaren mi entendimiento.

6—
Cantando me he de morir,
Cantando me han de enterrar,
Y cantando he de llegar
Al pie del Eterno Padre—
Dende el vientre de mi madre
Vine a este mundo a cantar.

13—
En el peligro ¡ qué Cristos!
El corazón se me enancha
Pues toda la tierra es cancha,
Y de esto naides se asombre,
El que se tiene por hombre
Donde quiera hace pata ancha.

14—
Soy gaucho, y entiendaló
Como mi lengua lo esplica,
Para mí la tierra es chica
Y pudiera ser mayor
Ni la víbora me pica
Ni quema mi frente el Sol.

17—
Yo no tengo en el amor
Quien me venga con querellas;
Como esas aves tan bellas
Que saltan de rama en rama—
Yo hago en el trébol mi cama,
Y me cubren las estrellas.

When I start my story
To refresh my memory
And illuminate my understanding.

6—
It's my destiny to die singing,
And be buried singing,
And singing I shall arrive
At the feet of the Eternal Father—
From my mother's womb
I came to this world to sing.

13—
In danger, Christ!
My heart swells,
For the whole earth is my battle-
    ground,—
Let none be surprised to hear
    this,—
He who holds himself a man
Puts up a fight anywhere.

14—
I'm a gaucho, and you must
    understand this
As my tongue explains it:
The earth is small for me,
And were it bigger,
The viper wouldn't bite me,
Nor the sun burn my brow.

17—
I have no beloved one
To come to me with upbraidings;
Like those birds so beautiful
Flitting from bough to bough,
I make my bed in the clover,
And the stars cover me.

—*Ida*, I

And now hear his verses on his daily life, as he herds cows and breaks horses on the ranch.

5—
Entonces—cuando el lucero
Brillaba en el cielo santo,
Y los gallos con su canto
Nos decían que el día llegaba,
A la cocina rumbiaba
El graucho. . . que era un encanto.

5—
Then—when the morning star
Twinkled in the peaceful sky,
And the cocks with their song
Told us day was coming,
Toward the kitchen
Headed the gaucho. . . 'twas a
    fine sight!

7—
Ya arpénas la madrugada
Empezaba a coloriar
Los pájaros a cantar,
Y las gallinas a apiarse,
Era cosa de largarse,
Cada cual a trabajar.

7—
And hardly had dawn
Begun to redden,
The birds to sing,
And the hens to leave their
    perch,
When it was time to set out,
Each one, to work.

8—
Este se ata las espuelas,
Sale el otro cantando,
Uno busca un pellón blando,
Este un lazo, otro un rebenque
Y los pingos relinchando
Los llaman dende el palenque.

8—
Here one is buckling on his
    spurs,
And another goes out singing,
One seeks a soft saddle-skin,
One a lasso, another a whip,
And the horses neighing
Call them from the hitching-post.

12—
Ah tiempos! era un orgullo
Ver ginetiar un paisano—
Cuando era gaucho baquiano
Aunque el potro se boliase,
No había uno que no parase
Con el cabestro en la mano.

12—
Ah! what times! it made one
    proud
To see a gaucho's horsemanship:
When he was a scout,
Even if his stallion had a fall
There wasn't a man who wouldn't
    light on his feet,
Halter in hand.

13—

Y mientras domaban unos,
Otros al campo salían,
Y la hacienda recogían,
Las manadas repuntaban,
Y ansí sin sentir pasaban
Entretenidos el día.

13—

And while some broke horses,
Others went out on the plain
And collected the herds
Or guided the flocks,
And so, unconcernedly, they
 would pass
The whole day happily.

14—

Y verlos al cair la noche
En la cocina riunidos,
Con el juego bien prendido
Y mil cosas que contar,
Platicar muy divertidos
Hasta despues de cenar.

14—

And to see them, at nightfall,
Gathered in the kitchen,
With the fire well lit
And a thousand things to tell,
Chat very merrily
Till after supper!

16—

Ricuerdo! . . . Qué maravilla!
Como andaba la gauchada,
Siempre alegre y bien montada
Y dispuesta pa el trabajo. . .
Pero hoy en el día. . . barajo
No se le vé de aporriada.

    —*Ida*, II

16—

I remember! . . . What a marvel!
How the gauchos were then:
Always happy and well mounted,
Ready for work—
But today, thunder!
They show it no more, so
 whipped are they.

"The nostalgia of that better age heightens by contrast the sad reality of the poem. 'Once I had, in my country, a wife, sons, and cattle,' says the *payador*, beginning the account of his family tragedy. He tells how he lost all that was dear, when the Justice of the Peace sent him arbitrarily, in a military contingent, to a certain frontier cantonment. He paints the sordid life of the fort, and the periodical invasions of the Indians. The picaresque color of the first picture contrasts with the tone of the second, for he now enters fully into the epic field, describing an Indian attack in more than a hundred lines."[3]

---

3. Rojas, *Op. cit.*, 483–484.

46—

Y pa mejor de la fiesta
En esa aflicción tan suma,
Vino un indio echando espuma,
Y con la lanza en la mano
Gritando: "Acabau cristiano
Metau el lanza hasta el pluma."

47—

Tendido en el costillar
Cimbrando por sobre el brazo
Una lanza como un lazo
Me atropelló dando gritos—
Si me descuido. . . el maldito
Me levanta de un lanzazo.

48—

Si me atribulo, o me encojo,
Siguro que no me escapo:
Siempre he sido medio guapo
Pero en aquella ocasión
Me hacía buya el corazón
Como la garganta al sapo.

—*Ida*, III

46—

And as the finishing touch
In our supreme distress,
An Indian came foaming,
With lance in hand,
Shrieking: "I'll end this Christian!
I'll stick my lance in him, up to
    the plume!"

47—

Stretched out on his horse's side,
And brandishing over his arm
His lance as if 'twere a lasso,
He closed with me, uttering yells!
If I'm careless—the knave
Will lift me with a lance-thrust!

48—

If I show fright, or shrink,
I'll surely not escape—
I've always been more or less bold,
But on that occasion
My heart kept knocking loudly
Like a frog's throat.

"After the fight, Fierro returns to cantonments and continues to brood over his misery: corporal punishment, nakedness, delayed pay, chiefs compelling privates to work for them and depriving them of their share of booty, trickery and fraud of the Italian storekeeper, upheld by the commandant, the police commissioner, and the judge (*Ida*, IV–VI) . . . Weary of the life, Fierro deserts. Returning to his home, he finds it a ruin, and his wife and sons dispersed by the very hardships his absence had caused them. Now the hero. . . breaks into heartrending sobs of human despair, revealing to what hidden depths of his soul the pangs of his manly grief penetrate. They who have said that the gaucho felt no love for his family, ought to re-read the elegy. . . of his abandoned home and companion whom he was fated never to see again. Out of his grief came the decision to become an outlaw. Henceforth his life[4] should be a militant protest. . . His exploit is the protest of a free man, in the midst of an embryonic democracy and virgin nature. . ."[5]

Cantos IX–XIII, the last of *La Ida*, recount the adventures of Martín Fierro as an outlaw after killing a negro at a certain gaucho festivity, and a local bully in a *pulpería*. His solitary nights in the desert, his encounter with the police riders and victory over them, his friendship with Cruz arising from that fight against odds—such are the principal themes of these Cantos.

Our hardy frontiersman having become an avowed outlaw, the casual reader will not look for demonstrations of tenderness, for the free course of the softer emotions. But let him read the following:

7—
Y al campo me iba solito,
Más matrero que el venao—
Como perro abandonao
A buscar una tapera,
O en alguna viscachera
Pasar la noche tirao.

7—
And I would roam the plain alone,
Wilder than the deer,
Like a deserted dog
Seeking a ruined house,
Or in a vizcacha's hole
Going to lie through the night.

8—
Sin punto ni rumbo fijo
En aquella inmensidá
Entre tanta oscuridá
Anda el gaucho como duende,
Allí jamás lo sorpriende
Dormido, la autoridá.

8—
With no fixed spot or goal
In that immense expanse,
In that great darkness,
The gaucho goes like a spook;
Never will he be caught there
Asleep, by the authorities.

9—
Su esperanza es el coraje,
Su guardia es la precautión,
Su pingo es la salvatión,
Y pasa uno en su desvelo,
Sin más amparo que el cielo
Ni otro amigo que el facón.

9—
His hope lies in his courage,
His guard is precaution.
His swift horse is his salvation,
And one thus passes his vigil
Without other defence than heaven,
Or other friend than his sword.

---

4. Like that of the hero of Schiller's *Die Räuber*.
5. Rojas, *Op. cit.*, 485–6.

10—

Ansí me hallaba una noche
Contemplando las estrellas
Que le parecen más bellas
Cuanto uno es más desgraciao,
Y que Dios las haiga criao
Para consolarse en ellas.

10—

And so I happened one night
To be gazing at the stars,
Which seem more lovely
The more one is unfortunate;
As if God made them
For one's consolation.

13—

Es triste en medio del campo
Pasarse noches enteras
Contemplando en sus carreras
Las estrellas que Dios cría,
Sin tener más compañía
Que su soledá y las fieras.
—*Ida*, IX

13—

It's sad in the midst of the plain
To pass whole nights
Watching in their courses
The stars that God creates,
With no other company
Than one's own loneliness and
the wild animals.

Martín does not say how many were in the party of gendarmes who thought to capture him the very night he was star-gazing. Probably there were not less than ten, of whom it looks as if at least three were "sent to the hole" (killed), and others badly wounded. Absurdly exaggerated prowess? Possibly, but I find, after many readings, that I note less the numbers, and much more the circumstances, so favorable to the gaucho, and so naturally, so convincingly interjected by Hernández between the various encounters.

The best feature of this Canto IX, that which lingers in the memory, is the generous, chivalrous action of the police sergeant, Cruz, who was so struck by Martín's valor that he changed sides, and helped the gaucho put his own platoon to flight. The poem is vastly enriched by the friendship thus abruptly formed. This companionship of two kindred souls, unshaken by all the buffetings of Fate, is epic, Spanish, and, as we have already seen, a requisite in Argentine gaucho literature. Cruz tells Martín how he happened to be in command of the police. Olympian humor punctuates this masterly stroke of the author's, for Cruz, we hear, had himself been an outlaw gaucho, whom the authorities had been anxious to reconcile to the social order. Consequently, they freely pardoned him and made him a sergeant to boot. They had need of a daring fellow, on the principle of "set a thief. . . !" (*Ida*, X–XII.)

This narration finished, Fierro begins in his turn, as the two gauchos leave behind them the scene of the fight. But Fierro is not inclined to waste time over the past. Rather, his proposal concerns the immediate present.

1—
Ya veo somos los dos
Astillas del mesmo palo—
Yo paso por gaucho malo
Y usté anda del mesmo modo,
Y yo, pa acabarlo todo,
A los Indios me refalo.

1—
I see well enough that we both
Are splinters from the same
   stick—
Folks call me a bad gaucho
And you're a lot like me:
And to be done with all this
I'm going over to the Indians.

2—
Pido perdón a mi Dios
Que tantos bienes me hizo—
Pero dende que es preciso
Que viva entre los infieles—
Yo seré cruel con los crueles—
Ansí mi suerte lo quiso.

2—
I ask forgiveness of my God,
Who has done me so many favors;
But since I must
Live among the heathen
I'll be cruel with the cruel:
So my fate has willed it.

—*Ida*, XIII

The ex-sergeant agrees to flee with Fierro to the Indians, and the lately made friends "rustle" some horses from a ranch and head for the frontier. This term sounds vague, just as we have seen that there is a vagueness as to the exact site of Martín's home in Buenos Aires Province. If, during his *matrero* period, he had hovered over some spot or spots of his home district, which I will call for convenience' sake, the Olavarría-Ayacucho-Tandil district,[6] then when absolutely forced to flee, as now, he would most probably aim southwest-by-south, to attain his objective most expeditiously. The question of the exact location of the frontier is discussed briefly in another chapter, but where our author is not careful to fix localities, it is to be feared that his readers cannot fix them, either.

Y cuando la habían pasao,
Una madrugada clara,
Le dijo Cruz que mirára

And when they had crossed the
   frontier,
At dawn of a clear day,

---

6. These are towns fairly far south in the Province.

Las últimas poblaciones,
Y a Fierro dos lagrimones
Le rodaron por la cara.

—*Ida*, XIII

Cruz bade him look
At the last settlements.
And Fierro felt two big tears
Roll down his face.

Cruz and Fierro, on arriving at an Indian village[7] live through some highly dramatic moments, but are ultimately rescued from the threatening weapons and informed that the *cacique* has decided to show them mercy (*Vu*, II). They are, however, quite closely guarded for a time, and even after this probationary period has passed, the savages exercise a surveillance over their self-invited guests. Perhaps this inherent suspiciousness, concomitant so many times of basest cruelty, accounts for part of Fierro's prejudice, visible in all his Indian story. In other words, he commenced his Indian life under discouraging auspices. And gloominess was to change into grief most intense, with the passing of Cruz at the time of the plague. Neither artistically nor naturally could any remedy exist for such grief, save in the return to the native land. But while Martín lived in the village, he had his eyes open, and he describes graphically the Indian life.[8] Their preserver was always kind, but in general they lived in the midst of filth, superstition, cruelty, and bestiality.

Days pass, the black pox comes, and Cruz is a victim. Martín in his loneliness is inconsolable. By his friend's grave, and in aimless walks, he pours out his grief (*Vu*, VI–VII).

One day he stumbles on a pampa atrocity (*Vu*, VIII). A white woman captive is being tortured, and her wee son has been killed, by the Indian master, in order that she may confess to having used witchcraft.[9]

---

7. The action, from this point, is related in *La Vuelta de Martín Fierro*.

8. *Vu*, II–VI, which, with the following four Cantos, form the basis of the study of the Indians, in Chapt. VII.

9. It was inhumanity to women which had already drawn from Fierro this eloquent tribute to their sex:

No se hallará una mugger
A la que esto no le cuadre—
Yo alabo al Eterno Padre,—
No porque las hizo bellas,
Sino porque a todas ellas
Les dió corazón de madre.

—*Vu*, V

You'll not find a woman
To whom this won't apply:
I praise God,
Not that he made them fair,
But that to every one of them
He gave a mother-heart.

At this moment, the sad, scornful mood leaves Martín Fierro, and in its stead there surges up a feeling not dissimilar to that which must have swayed those Spaniards who, their backs to the Asturian hills, upheld the cross against the warriors of Islam in the days of Pelayo the Goth. One instant, he faced the Indian, and their hostile glances crossed; the next, they were engaged in a life and death struggle. Providentially, as it appears to the gaucho, he won (*Vu*, IX), but after killing the brave, he must flee for his life; he takes the white woman along, and the tale of their crossing the desert, back to the white settlements, is absorbing (*Vu*, X). Back again in so-called civilization, he bids farewell to his protégée, and passes from one ranch to another, seeking his old friends. Some of these inform him that Justice is no longer "camping on his trail." A greater satisfaction comes when, at a certain gaucho gathering, the hero meets two of his sons again. This reunion makes the simple festivities truly memorable. Seated among friends, Martín tells his tale, bringing it up to date for them and for his sons, who then sing of their experiences since all their father's land and cattle were seized by rascals of cunning speech, and they themselves were compelled, in their youth and poverty, to "hire out" on neighboring ranches (*Ida*, VI). Now they are men, schooled by many a hard and bitter knock (*han vivido padeciendo*, says *Vu*, XI). The older of the two had been unjustly sent to the penitentiary. While he was employed on a certain cattle-ranch, a neighboring rancher had been murdered, and evil men had the charge brought to young Fierro's door. Apparently, he had not been long out of prison, when he meets his father. The account of the soul-travail in the penitentiary is moving (*Vu*, XII).

His brother's is a longer story, which would not profoundly interest us were it not for his association with Viscacha, an old thief and rascal who was named his guardian and who robbed him of his scanty belongings. The portrait of Viscacha is unusually well drawn.[10]

A young stranger calling himself at first "Picardía," begs to be admitted to the circle around Fierro and his sons. He too proves to be a very fair singer. Ultimately we learn that he is that son of Cruz, whom the latter on his deathbed entrusted to Martín, should providence ever bring the two together. Picardía has followed many callings, all disreputable; but just recently he has learned who his father was, and

---

10. But it is perhaps unfortunate for art that the second son's story fills seven cantos. Say what the kindly critic may, a canto or two might well have been omitted.

it has made a different being of him. (*Vu*, XX–XXVIII). Here, then, is what might be a happy group, but news of his wife's death (*Vu*, XI), prevents Martín from making any demonstration. His is the gaucho philosophy! However, a moment of peace sheds a subdued radiance over even the previous events that have fashioned them what they are.

All these have had their turn, singing to the guitar. Enters an ebon-skinned bard, who does not ask permission to participate, but obviously challenges Fierro to a *canto de contrapunto*, or trial of their respective abilities as *payadores*. The singing takes place in Canto XXX, and the occasion gives birth to some very beautiful lyric verse. The theme is "The song of the night."

30—
La noche por cantos tiene
Esos ruidos que uno siente
Sin saber por dónde vienen.

30—
For songs, night has
Those noises one hears
Without knowing whence they
    come.

31—
Son los secretos misterios
Que las tinieblas esconden—
Son los écos que responden
A la voz que dá un grito,
Como un lamento infinito
Que viene no sé de donde.

31—
They are the secret mysteries
Hidden by darkness—
They are the echoes answering
The voice that cries aloud,
Like an infinite lament
Coming I know not whence.

32—
En distintas direcciones
Se oyen rumores inciertos,
Son almas de los que han muerto
Que nos piden oraciones.
    —*Vu*, XXX

32—
In different quarters
You may hear uncertain sounds:
It's the souls of the dead
Who are begging our prayers.

Smarting from his defeat in this trial, the negro informs Martín that he is a brother of the man whom Martín killed years before at the dance. The situation is difficult: Fierro is not in a mood to wish to exculpate himself, but the threat in his opponent's words is scarcely veiled. The story does, therefore, exactly what you and I would do under the circumstances. It temporizes. Friends see to it that the two parties are drawn off in opposite directions, and—we shall never know how this question of vengeance is settled!

For now the story reaches its close. Fierro gives some excellent advice to his sons and Picardía, and each of the four goes his separate way. There would not be bread enough for all in any one establishment to which they might apply. In Canto XXXIII, Hernández speaks for himself. The sermon so oft on the lips of Cruz, Fierro, and the rest, is reiterated. The gauchos should have their rights,[11] education, religious advantages.

The scene is one of comparative tranquillity. The gaucho had not succeeded in life, but he had borne suffering unflinchingly, and he had finally come to a sort of haven. We cannot rebel against the conclusion, because from the many "asides" of Hernández, it is evident that the plainsmen, as a social unit, had to expect penury, persecution, and prompt extinction. What lot befell Martín, individually, each reader may imagine for himself. Without doubt each would wish for him at least some sunshine after so many storms, so many wrongs—

> *Y ya con estas noticias*
> *Mi relación acabé,*
> *Por ser ciertas las conté*
> *Todas las desgracias dichas,*
>
> *. . . . .*
>
> *Pero ponga su esperanza*
> *En el Dios que lo formó.*
> *Y que me despido yo*
> *Que he relatao a mi modo*
> *Males que conocen todos*
> *Pero que naides cantó.*[12]

—*Ida*, XIII

11.
> *Debe el gaucho tener casa,*
> *Escuela, iglesia, y derechos.*

—*Loc. cit.* Cf. *Ida*, XII, *et passim*

12.
> *And now, with this*
> *My tale is ended.*
> *Because they're true I've told*
> *All the misfortunes aforesaid.*
>
> *. . . . .*

But let him (i.e., the gaucho) hope
In God who made him.
And now I bid you farewell.
Having told in my own way
Wrongs that everyone knows
But which none as yet has sung.

HENRY A. HOLMES AND JOSÉ HERNÁNDEZ

VI

The Gaucho in "Martín Fierro"

I n this chapter I shall not feel called upon to describe all the details
of gaucho life, nor even cite all those sung in *Martín Fierro*. Let us
concentrate on the most "synthetic" passages—not necessarily the most
beautiful, but the most revealing.

At the outset the reader may be informed that not all gauchos were,
like Fierro, *cantores* blest with superabundant humor and pathos. Not
every gaucho would have a tale of woe to tell. As a class, however, the
plainsmen and their families were distinguished for their humor, sly
more often than boisterous, always pungent; and for their rich vein of
melancholy. Nor is it less true that large numbers were the butt of cruel
and conscienceless elements in the Argentine society of that day. Thus
the rhapsody of Fierro over the old gaucho days is to be considered, if
not an exaggeration, at least an example of the voluntary blindness, the
glad forgetfulness which master us all when, to use the cant phrase, we
worship at memory's shrine.[1] The glamour of his past owed something
to the afflictions of his present.

Martín proudly enumerates the fine gaucho trappings he possessed
when he rode away to the frontier:[2] saddlecloths, poncho, leather thongs,
headstalls, halter, lasso, *bolas*, and hobbling-strap. Be assured that he too
was bedecked, and rode a racer, a proud "mane-tosser." It will help us to
grasp depths and values in this poem, if we picture Martín to ourselves
as no beggar in those days. He has just said that he was a happy husband
and father, with a good gaucho home, and some livestock. Note this last:
he had perhaps a certain economic independence. So had the hero of
Gutiérrez' novel, *Juan Moreira*. Such men were unusually circumstanced,
I grant, but the times had been very patriarchal. Nobody, not even the
wealthiest landowners, enjoyed such luxury as consider that no bridgeless
gulf separated his condition we know of, today, and a humble gaucho
might easily from that of his *patrón*. The tales of Godofredo Daireaux

---

1. *Ida,* I.
2. *Ida,* III.

in *Tipos y Paisajes*[3] offer evidence in support of this. A tragedy is lying in wait for this picturesque fellow as he kisses his *china*, and rides too lightheartedly away to the rendezvous of conscripts!

The gaucho attire was indeed unique. References to it in *Martín Fierro* are very numerous. See especially Cantos IV, VIII, and IX of *La Ida*. Over his shirt the gaucho threw a *poncho* or ample cape, in reality a blanket, with an opening for the head in the center. It was made of *vicuña* wool. The term *poncho* is Araucanian. He wrapped around waist and legs the *chiripá* (a Kechuan word), a strip of black baize. Beneath this, in turn, were cotton drawers. Horsehide boots and huge spurs were *de rigueur*. But the poor, especially the negroes, used *tamangos*, rude boots made of remnants of hides.[4] Around his supple waist was passed a wide sash. Now let him trick himself out with silver buttons, and possibly silver in his other gear, and put a *chambergo*, or wide-brimmed *sombrero* on his head: behold the lord of the plains! The women's dress was not so picturesque. The gowns were of print cotton, or of wool, with numerous petticoats as a basis. Loose wrappers called *batas* were and are customary. For gala occasions, brilliant bits of color appeared in the shape of scarves, ribbons, or shawls, and jewelry might be displayed. In the privacy of the *rancho*, shoes and stockings were dispensed with, and the *china* "flipflopped" about her rounds in *alpargatas* or hemp sandals. Naturally, slippers and stockings were a *summum desideratum* of the better-situated *china*, for state occasions. Bonnets were unknown to this class, but when headgear was required, the *manta*, a thin black scarf, was both useful and graceful. For wraps, did not the poncho serve both male and female?

Little does Martín foresee into what kind of existence the government, anxiously and often ingloriously defending the frontier against the Indians, is about to throw him! And yet—if he is not in his own element at the frontier, who, pray, would be? Consider the essentials: his house is the open field, his food—[5]

> *Se come uno hasta las colas*
> *Cuando se anda en el desierto.*

> —*Ida*, XIII

---

3. Especially in the *Fourth Series,* 1903.
4. *Ida,* VII.
5.   *You eat even the tails (of animals killed on the pampa)*
          When you cross the desert.

his drink (in the dire case that a flask of gin were lacking)—[6]

> *Ande hay duraznillo blanco*
> *Cabo, y la saco (i.e., water) al momento.*
>
> —*Ibid*

his bed—[7].

> *Más siguro que en su rancho*
> *Uno ronca a pierna suelta,*
> *Pues en el suelo no hay chinches.*
>
> —*Vu*, XXXII

his friend, best defense, and mode of conveyance—a good horse.

All gaucho poetry, as you fould expect, teems with allusions to the horse. In *Martín Fierro* they are so numerous as to make citations unnecessary. Read any canto. One of the finest touches, so brief as to be easily overlooked, is the line where Martín says that, just before fighting the police, he took his stand, backed up against his horse.[8] Rojas[9] gives thirty-three gaucho terms of equitation. From Segovia's *Diccionario de Argentinismos*[10] I have gathered a still longer list. The works of Javier de Viana (e.g., *Gaucha*) and of other creole writers, are sources. Of the hundred or more "horse" terms I have found, many indicate the color, as *colorado* (chestnut); others swiftness, as *parejero* (race-horse); still others, habits, as *volvedor* (horse fond of returning home); and, finally, others denote condition, as *maceta* (old or overworked).

And should his steed give out, and his good *cuchillo* (short sword, also called *facón*) as well, the gaucho was an expert in the use of the *bolas*. How often they are mentioned! The *bolas*, or, in slang, *las tres Marías*[11]

---

6.   *Where there's a white peach-tree*
                     I dig, and get water at once.
7.   *More secure than in his house*
                     One snores profoundly.
             For on the ground there are no bedbugs!
8. *Ida,* IX.
9. *Op. cit.,* 339–340 N.
10. *Sección Campaña.*
11. *Ida,* III, XIII; *Vu,* IV, XVII; *et passim.*

(after the constellation of Orion), were a favorite weapon of the Indians, who had no tomahawk like their North American confrères. Sometimes there were only two, sometimes three balls, of metal or stone, joined the one to the other by cords. It seems from what Martín says in *Ida*, III and *Vu*, IX, that an adept could deliver with them a blow as fatal at close range as that of a bullet.[12]

We are told by Lugones that the *bolas* were also hurled in such a way as to trip up an animal or man.[13] When there were three cords, he continues, one ball, on a taut cord, was kept between the bare toes (he seems to imply the fighter was an Indian!), and the other two were held or whirled at the height of the head, and discharged together. The gaucho did not disdain, on occasion, another Indian weapon, the long cane lance.

Coming after the gaucho's arms and mount to his wife,—an order of relative values far from rare on the pampa—it must be confessed that there is no Helen of Troy in *Martín Fierro*. The few women depicted are all nameless. Had the weaker sex played a more prominent rôle in Martín's thinking, we should have had not merely these very worthy but scanty verses, but also much more epic action by Martín's wife, or some other woman or women. The one heroic act in the whole poem to be credited to a woman is that performed by the Christian captive in Canto IX of *La Vuelta*, She saved Martín's life in his fight with the Indian, by dragging the latter off Martín's prostrate body. The deed is the finest among many supremely fine details which make this combat one to thrill us in memory. This woman is of the same fighting blood as Kriemhilde of the *Nibelungenlied*. She crosses the desert with Martín[14] and, so far as we know, the conventions are observed, if not exactly as Mrs. Grundy would insist. Reaching the white man's land, she shifts for herself. Of such pioneer men and women are born the nations of America!

But Fierro's wife was not like the Christian captive, nor was the wife of Cruz. Both men praise woman, and sincerely. Nevertheless, their praise is incomplete, concerning itself with but two or three phases of that complex: a woman's nature. Notoriously, the women of the most

---

12.   *Si lo alcanza, sin vida*
        Es siguro que lo deja.

13. *Op. cit.*, 231–2.

14. *Ida*, X.

degraded savage tribes toil for their lords, nurse them, and will not desert them. Can Cruz in his praise go no further than this, or the sentimental recollection of physical charms? No.[15]

> Yo también tuve una pilcha
> Que me enllenó el corazón,
> Y si en aquella ocasión
> Alguien me hubiera buscado—
> Siguro que me había hallao
> Más prendido que un botón.
>
> . . . .
>
> Si es güena, no lo abandona
> Cuando lo vé desgraciao,
> Lo asiste con su cuidao,
> Y con afán cariñoso
> Y usté tal vez ni un rebozo
> Ni una pollera le ha dao.
>
> . . . .
>
> Era la aguila que a un arbol
> Dende las nubes bajó
> Era mas linda que el alba
> Cuando va rayando el sol—

15.
> I too once had a treasure
> Who made my heart full to the brim,
> And if in those days
> Any one had been looking for me,
> It's sure he would have found me
> Attached to her tighter than a button.
>
> . . . .
>
> If she is good she won't leave you
> When she sees you in straits,
> She stands by you devotedly
> And with love's zeal,
> And it may be you've not given her
> So much as a mantle or a skirt.
>
> . . . .
>
> She was the eagle which came
> From the clouds to me, the tree,
> Lovelier than the dawn
> When the sun shoots his first rays—
> She was the delightsome flower
> Growing amid the clover.

Era la flor deliciosa
Que entre el trevolar creció.

—*Ida*, X

The tribute of Martín[16] is more discerning, yet it is confessedly inadequate, and in the confession is seen the hand of the author. The point I seek to make is, that there is a direct relationship between the gaucho estimate of woman and the part played in *Martín Fierro* by woman. For Fierro and his like, the *china* was emphatically the home-keeping companion, laborious, but ignorant and insignificant when great events were toward.

What else could a woman be but a hewer of wood and a drawer of water—and a bearer of strong offspring? The conception of woman as the equal of these strong men would by them have been judged fantastic. In *Martín Fierro* woman is pictured as an excellent playmate,[17] deserving of a home, and entitled to gain its security as best she might,[18] tender-hearted, and—to be treated with vast discretion![19]

Siempre los ha de perder
Una mujer ofendida.

—*Vu*, XXXIII

When the creole dishes were called for, such as the *mazamorra* (a species of pudding made with crushed hominy), the *came con cuero*, or meat roasted in the hide, the *carbonada*, or meat stew (with several vegetables cooked with the meat), the *puchero* or "boiled dinner," the many savory concoctions with rice, corn, squash, onions, and other vegetables, the *pasteles* or pasties, the *rellenos* or stuffed fowls, the cheeses, fried cakes, and many another tidbit,—then, at least, there was no question of the feminine supremacy.[20]

---

16. *Vu*, V.
17. *Ida*, VII, X, XI.
18. *Ida*, VI.
19.   *You're always sure to be ruined*
        By an offended woman.

20. Cf. *Ida*, II.

The general conclusions which have been reached in the foregoing, do not preclude the possible existence of unusual *paisanos* here and there. That there were exceptions to whom woman was a companion rightly esteemed and cherished, is not to be doubted. Possibly the author of *Calandria* implies that the outlaw Servando is to turn into this exceptional type.

But it is certainly suggestive of a certain indifference, laxity—what you will—that Martín does not condemn his wife for going off with an unknown gallant, during his absence! There is thus a varying mood with respect to women.[21] With an epic superiority and insouciance the gauchos dance and flirt with the *chinas*, at certain *fiestas*,[22] and yet there are described other gatherings at which there is not a suggestion that women were present:[23] these latter were just as successful from our friends' point of view. There is no implication that gaucho women shared the gaming-bouts. Rather, it seems well-nigh certain they did not, given the frequent sanguinary finishes of such diversions.

Other works, such as the *Calandria* already mentioned, and *Montaraz* of the same author, deal in more detailed fashion with gaucho amusements. In the former,[24] racing and dicing are described; in the latter,[25] the game of the *sortijas*, a Spanish-Moorish contest,[26] centuries old, and still popular, wherein various horsemen at full speed endeavor to bear away a suspended iron ring on their lances' points, and the "flag-rush," which is played on horseback. Beauty was usually present, to smile on displays of valor. Mitre, in his *Armonías de la Pampa*,[27] describes the game of the *pato*, a kind of tug-of-war played on horseback. So too does W. H. Hudson in the appendix to a fascinating collection of short stories entitled *El Ombú*. Cock-fights and ostrich hunts were very popular. In Canto II of *La Ida*, the sheep-shearing and cattle-branding bring together at the same ranch gauchos from far and near, who throw the whole feminine side of the establishment into disarray with the

---

21. Cf. *Ida*, VII, XIII; *Vu*, VII, XX: the relation of the extremely pious aunts who tried to catechize Picardía; and *Vu*, XIX: an unlucky passion for a widow.

22. *Ida*, VII, XI.

23. *Ida*, VIII; *Vu*, X.

24. 161 ff.

25. 246 ff.

26. Not confined to Spain. It was also played in France. It is referred to in the *Encyclopedia of Sports*, Philadelphia, 1911, vol. III, 181. It is not unknown in Maryland today. See files of *Baltimore Sun* for August, 1922.

27. Included in his *Rimas*, 123 ff.

unusual demands, culinary and social. The social part played by music on such occasions has already been intimated.

Even if a gaucho were or might be revengeful, lonely, and in abject poverty, he still enjoyed the country dances. Going to them seems to have been a favorite pastime of the gaucho outlaws.[28] A house or tavern might be so mean, so unprepossessing, as to merit the opprobrious qualification of *casa de mala muerte,* but thither the gauchos for miles around would resort for festivity. Is a man struck down in some obscure affray? hoist him up, quick! on the wine-casks! there's no other free spot in the reeking room. Lugones, out of an experience of surprising range, affirms that he has often seen wounded men so treated.[29]

One such reunion to which Martín repaired was fateful for him. A negro appeared, with his dusky damsel. Martín was not sober. Probably, too, it was the custom of his class to speak jestingly of negroes. Toward the end of *La Vuelta*, we have another illustration of this, in phrases of the *payada.* If Martín was tipsy, the Africans were uppish as they joined in the merry-making: *va-ca-yendo gente al baile.* And like all children of nature, the gauchos were intensely narrow. . .

Their challenge was often tricked out in intense sarcasm. To save their lives (or lose them), they would not have omitted the verbal parade, as a Guerra or a Fuentes would not omit any iota of the ceremony of the Spanish bullring. No courtesies are wanting at Martín's duel. Even as the blades are about to cross, the "gentlemen" bystanders are begged to make room: *Caballeros, dejen venir ese toro.*[30] The *facón* or long broad-bladed dagger, with S-shaped hilt-guard, has inspired Bunge to distinguish sharply between the *capa y espada* duels of Spain and those of the gauchos.[31] Some critics there are, as Lugones, who would take issue with him. However that may be, it is useless to deny the gauchos a certain flavor of *hidalguía.* Canto XI of *La Vuelta* shows conclusively that Martín and his fellows had clear ideas as to what was the honorable duel and what the dishonorable.

The perfect gaucho is as little insincere as he is a coward. His virtues are not complex, but genuine. How terribly the world's verdict sears the

---

28. *Ida,* VIII. Cf. *Ida,* XI and *Calandria,* 153–170.

29. *Op. cit.,* 170.

30. Cf. Roldán: *Bajo la toca de lino,* 55. *Te olvidabas que sos m'hijo,* says one duellist to the other.

31. *Op. cit.,* Introd., 30–35.

gaucho heart, as much sinned against as sinning, we hear in Fierro's outburst after two duelling experiences:[32]

El gaucho en esta tierra
Solo sirve pa votar.
Para el son los calabozos,
Para el las duras prisiones.

. . . .

Si uno aguanta es gaucho bruto,
Si no aguanta es gaucho malo,
Dele azote, dele palo!
Porque es lo que el necesita!
De todo el que nacio gaucho
Esta es la suerte maldita.

—*Ida,* VIII

What remedy save that of flight, applying to the heart's bruises the chilly balm of a crude but virile philosophy? Says Cruz:[33]

Con tanto padecer
Malicio que he de tener
Un callo en el corazón.

—*Ida,* XI

---

32.   *The gaucho in this land*
       Is only good to cast a vote.
       For him are the prisons.
       For him the cruel bonds.

       . . . .

       If one endures, he's a brute,
       If one resists, he's a bad gaucho;
       Give him stripes, cudgellings!
       That's what he needs!
       Of every one born a gaucho
       This is the damnable lot.

33.   *After so much suffering*
       I suspect I must have
       A callus on my heart!

His stoicism, in other words, was not born, but made. Previously he had said:[34]

> *Hagámosle cara fiera*
> *A los males, compañero,*
> *Porque el zorro más matrero*
> *Suele caír como un chorlito.*
> *Viene por un cordcrito,*
> *Y en la estaca deja el cuero.*

> —*Ida*, X

We are impressed by the rough fatalism of those who daily witness tragedies, on the pampa about them, and in the lives of their fellow-men, but that first statement of Cruz was erroneous. Did he never think of his son, and did that son, Picardía, never long to know of his father? Even in this family, whose integrity had been wrecked by the sin of the mother, the paternal, the filial impulses are sweet and sound. And how Fierro loves, and counsels with, his sons! This is one of the details which attest the "Argentinidad," as Rojas would call it, of the work. Only of late has the young Argentine woman begun to play prominent parts in a well-rounded, up-to-date social system (now that she has begun, her progress is sure to be truly great); but yesterday, today and always, the Argentine father centers his pride in his son.

When Fierro and Cruz, murderers in the eyes of the police, crossed the frontier, they were under the spell of that—to them—memorable dawning. Blanketing darkness has been torn away—the pale light reveals their iron faces and forms—the confines are pushed ever farther back—the sun rushes up! The world with all its significance even for a persecuted gaucho, exists again, and on their part of it, they are deliberately turning their backs! It is a typical gaucho scene, for inward characteristics blend with outward in "one touch of nature," and Martín

---

34.
> *Let's put on a bold front*
> *Against these evils, friend!*
> *For the most cunning fox*
> *Gets caught like a chorlito*
> *(marsh bird, easily caught).*
> *He goes after a little lamb,*
> *And instead he leaves his own skin to dry on the stakes.*

does what any gaucho would do: he lets the hot tears roll down his cheeks unchecked.[35]

It would not have been a good time to jest with these twain! When the plainsman was sufficiently bloody beneath the bludgeonings of fate, but not bowed, he summoned his heart to a resolve worthy of the school of Calderón:[36]

> *Respetar tan sólo a Dios,*
> *De Dios abajo, a ninguno.*

If we feel a pang of sympathy for these mature men, how can we fail to pity the young convict son of Fierro? His wretchedness is added evidence that society's verdict against the Fierros has been thorough-going. Frontier and penitentiary were thus invoked against the *criollos*. The reader must not misunderstand this testimony. He must not imagine there was only one social class, the gauchos, in Argentina outside of Buenos Aires, nor that all gauchos were persecuted and became outlaws. Let him admit the inevitable in history and social evolution, and then give his sympathies wholly to those on the losing (and vanished) side, the side that could rope and tie a steer, but could not get a decent market value for him, that could dominate for years the vast plains, yet never realize their commercial possibilities. Let him for aesthetic reasons try to think their thoughts and feel as they then felt. They had, indeed, a weighty cause; let him proceed for the moment as if they alone had one.

There was one Commandant,[37] in charge of the conscription in which Picardía was caught, who was well aware of the popular detestation of such service. He tried to escape its odium by ascribing the levy to the Judge. The attempt was more or less vain! Nevertheless, we cannot feel the same antipathy for this man of blood and iron, performing a duty imposed by higher officialdom, that we feel for the *ñato*.[38] This fellow, as he was only a local official, was alternately a toady to his betters and a tyrant to those beneath him. Picardía was sent by him to the stocks in retaliation for almost involuntary taunts.[39] How fiendish is the *ñato's*

---

35. *Ida,* XIII.
36. 　　　　　　　　*To respect God alone,*
　　　　　　　　　　Below God, nobody.

37. *Vu,* XXV.
38. The term means that he had an abnormally flattened nose.
39. *Vu,* XXIV.

glee as, standing by the Commandant, he points out those whom he has enabled the police to catch in their drag-net![40]

Men of this type were unfortunately all too common, and to the elementary gaucho mind, they represented faithfully the superior officials, the judges, police *comisarios*, and military men whom they served. Small wonder that Martín's sort lumped together village bullies, city officials, and the cities whence the latter brought their harsh mandates. Such practices were foreign to the kindly, hearty spirit of the gauchos although they could perceive the baseness with sufficient clearness.

We gladly turn from these black pages, to those of Canto XXX of *La Vuelta*, where is described the famous *payada de contrapunto*. To anyone who has read the *tensons* of the Provençal poets, it will be sufficient to say that the *payada de contrapunto* is the gaucho *tenson*. The two interlocutors, each of whom has a stanza, more or less, in turn, discuss problems amorous, metaphysical, religious, satirical or otherwise, and the better singer is declared the victor. Larousse's definition of the *tenson* will apply marvellously well to Canto XXX: "One of them executed a prelude, proposed the theme, and sang a stanza; the other in turn sang, in the same rhythm and to the same air, a response to the preceding strophe. . . These dialogues were mostly improvised."[41] It is a far cry from the courts of the languorous chatelaines of Provence, to the squalid taverns of the pampa, but music hath power as well as charms.

Only a genuine *cantor* or *payador*, one who could compose his own song, on the spot, was capable of sustaining a part with credit in these *tours de force*, the delight of the cowboys. Did such a singer triumph, his glory was great, and if he repeated his triumph often enough, the fame of it would extend beyond his own *pago* (locality), so that challengers would come to him, and he might be sure of a rousing welcome wherever he might wander. Some of the famous gaucho *payadores* did indeed wander far and wide, singing like blind Homer or those other and lesser blind ballad singers of Spain. The matches seem to have been

---

40. Y allí las pobres hermanas,   And there the poor sisters.
   Las madres y las esposas   The mothers, and wives
   Redamaban cariñosas   Were shedding, because of their love,
   Sus lágrimas de dolor.   Tears of grief.
       —*Vu*, XXV

41. Larousse, *Dictionnaire:* s. v. *Tenson.*

generally *à l'outrance,* and there is in Canto XXXI[42] an indication, amply sustained in other works, that from wooing the muse, the minstrels turned sometimes to following Bellona, goddess of strife! The contest between Martín and the negro, notable from the literary standpoint, is elsewhere discussed. Not infrequently *payadas* lasted whole nights through. *Las trasnochadas no acobardan,*[43] says Fierro, and a lengthy *payada,* with many a keen sally and biting allusion, before one singer had to acknowledge his inferiority in words or music, or both, was all the greater treat to the audience.

Sarmiento, in his *Facundo,* says the other South American countries think of Argentina as an especially musical nation. They said to him, or some compatriot, in Chile: "Being an Argentine, you must be musical."[44] While there are no similar direct assertions in *Martín Fierro,* there are a number of implications. It may not be surprising that Fierro's sons should follow their gifted father in singing to the guitar, but we feel it rather more than a coincidence that Cruz too should say:[45]

> *A otros les brotan las coplas*
> *Como agua de manantial;*
> *Pues a mí me pasa igual.*
>
> —*Ida,* XI

that his son should sing so entertainingly, that the *ñato* should be a singer, and so on through this and other gaucho narratives.[46]

These rude men, in their lyric contest, have constant recourse to Nature as they know her. We are now slightly acquainted with the Nature rôle in the poem. In frequent re-readings, this rôle takes on greater and greater proportions. Nature does not mean merely a certain landscape, a certain province, nor even merely this world. She is rather, to our gaucho friends, a great army of influences, with which they have

---

42. *Se pusieron de por medio,* etc.
43. Allnight sittings don't terrify.
44. *Facundo,* 70.
45.   *From others' lips the couplets gush*
                          Like spring water;
                      Well, the same thing happens to me.
46. It is no more amazing that they taught themselves the deepest secrets of the guitar's music, so thoroughly that this "simple" instrument swayed the auditors through all the varying forms and degrees of emotion, than that the Greek rhapsodists should master their lyre!

been long and intimately acquainted. They feel her force in the storm, and in the rush of the untamed steed. They sense her beauty in the stars that seem more lovely when one is in misfortune,[47] and in the profound maternal instinct of woman.[48] They feel her mystery in the loneliness of the desert.[49] And they draw from her unexplained processes their simple chaplet of popular sayings. They observe, for example:[50]

> *Siempre es dañosa la sombra*
> *Del arbol que tiene leche.*
>
> —*Vu*, XXXIII

Thrice-blessed be Sancho Panza, who, if he did not invent the proverb as a Spanish literary form, at any rate made this form immortal! Let him stand godfather to our gaucho personages who in the following proverbs *say something*, and say it unforgettably. For with the salt in the saying are mingled the inimitable wink, shrug, gesture, and the thousand and one other mannerisms of which the *criollos* have the copyright.

> *Esto es como en un nidal*
> *Echarle güebos a un gato.*[51]
>
> —*Ida*, V

> *Mañana será otro día.*[52]
>
> —*Ida*, X

> *Pa su agüela,*
> *Han de ser esas perdices.*[53]
>
> —*Ida*, X

---

47. *Ida*, IX.
48. *Vu*, V.
49. *Ida*, IX; cf. translation of this and above references, in the preceding chapter; *Vu*, V and X.
50.   *Ever think harmful the shade*
                            Of the tree that has milk.
                     (i.e., white fluid in branches or stalks.)
51. As silly as putting eggs under a cat.
52. Tomorrow's another day.
53. Those (sc. decayed) partridges must be for your grandmother.

Dejo rodar la bola
Que algún día ha de parar.[54]

—*Ida,* XII

Jamas llegués a parar,
A donde veas perros flacos.[55]

—*Vu,* XV

El diablo sabe por diablo
Pero más sabe por viejo.[56]

—*Ibid*

No dejés que hombre ninguno
Te gane el lao del cuchillo.[57]

—*Ibid*

Al que nace barrigón,
Es al ñudo que lo fagen.[58]

—*Ibid*

La miseria. . .
Llama en la puerta de todos
Y entra en la del haragan.[59]

—*Vu,* XXXII

Crisp and interest-gripping, in them are compressed Iberian joys and sorrows of a thousand years. Here blood speaks to blood that flowed in centuries gone by, and Martín Fierro shakes hands with Sancho Panza.

The following story, related to me by an Argentine colleague, must suffice to illustrate the readiness of gaucho wit, under any conditions.

---

54. Let the ball roll; some day it's got to stop.
55. Never stop (sc. at a house) where the dogs are thin.
56. The devil knows a lot because he's the devil, but more because he's old.
57. Never let anybody get the knife side of you (i.e., get the drop on you).
58. Useless to put a belt on a man born fat.
59. Poverty. . . knocks at every man's door, and enters that of the lasy man.

An old, old gaucho, of pungent wit but sadly evil habits, was brought down at last to his deathbed. To him, as he lay in this case, came an old acquaintance, his former *patrona,* an extremely pious lady, who deluged him with sombre homilies. At last the lady took her leave, and the gaucho's brother, entering the chamber, asked what had been the topic of conversation. "Oh," replied the dying man, "she wanted to make a round-up of all my sins!" (*Eya quería haserme un rodeo le tuítos mis pecaos!*)[60]

Naturally we wish to know what the gaucho's religion was. Men who, most of them, could not read or write their own names (*yo no soy cantor letrao,* says Fierro in the first Canto, which may or may not be taken to mean that he is illiterate; the probabilities are that he was), did not seek their spiritual guidance in books. They had not had much of it in any form. Baptized most of them had probably been,[61] but little else. There is no doubt they considered themselves children of the Roman

---

60. It is time that some authoritative philological study should dispel the notion that the language of Martín Fierro and his fellows is distinct from Spanish. What I have termed "the gaucho language" has for its base the Castellano of the sixteenth century colonists, which has been governed in Argentina by the same phonetic laws as those that have been operative in the mother country. Though there is an interesting Indian element in the gaucho vocabulary, the great majority of the words are of Spanish origin, even though a form may have been coined this side of the Atlantic, as (presumably) the augmentative *facón* (short sword, from *faca,* curved knife, cf. Latin *falx*).

Briefly, the gaucho vocabulary (in so far as it calls for comment) may be divided into:

1. The fund of *popular* forms, as *dotor, dueblen, ruempa* for *rompa, irüesos* for *huesos, juir* for *huir, culandrera* for *curandera* (a woman healer), *despedición* for *expedición,* etc.

2. The archaic forms, as *ansina* for *así. mesma, trujo, vía* for *veía, dende* for *desde alli,* etc. Of course, both of these types abound in the literature of Spain itself.

3. Those forms which may be styled *Argentinismos,* because they are:

A. Used with different meaning from that given to them in Spain, as *apero,* which in the *Diccionario de la Academia* means a collection of farming tools, and in Argentina the saddle and other trappings for a horseman; *pingo,* whose feminine form means, according to the *Diccionario,* a frivolous woman, and which in Argentina is used of a fast horse; *punteado,* referred by the *Diccionario* to the action of playing the guitar, and used in Argentina of a drunken man; *matrero,* signifying, according to the *Diccionario,* one who is astute and experienced, and in Argentina one who is wild or an outlaw.

B. Taken from various Indian languages, as *gaucho* (cf. Chapt. I), *iruasca,* a leather strip (from the Araucanian), *chajá,* a bird (Guaraní), *tape,* an Indian (Guaraní), *gualicho,* devil, and *chiripá,* the gaucho substitute for breeches (both these latter words from the Araucanian).

This vocabulary survives the gauchos themselves. Much of it is steadily used by great numbers of Argentines, though we must make exceptions over more numerous due to origin, rank, or education. Familiar speech will doubtless never be free from some of the picturesque expressions of *Martín Fierro.*

61. Cf. *Ida,* VIII: *Le echan la agua del bautismo.*

Church, but we do not hear Martín say once that he has attended mass or been to confession. Yet there were priests here and there through the country, as well as in all the larger settlements. Probably these made, as they now make, occasional rounds of the *estancias* to baptize and hold mass and hear confession. And it may be that Martín had been present now and then, but he hardly seems to lit in the category of the "church-goers!" Picardía was vainly catechized for a time by some extremely pious aunts.[62] He finally escaped from these well-meant exercises. The negro in *Vu*, XXX, professes to have been instructed by a priest. It is well to mention all this, in order to show that the Roman Church was thoroughly established, and that these gauchos called themselves sons of it. But after all, their religion is, as it were, accidental, external, shown in casual manifestations or in mechanical repetitions. There is a delightful touch in *Ida*, IX, after that Titanic fight with the gendarmes, in which one man did much execution, in truth. Martín says:[63]

> *Yo junté las osamentas,*
> *Me hinqué y les recé un bendito;*
> *Hice una cruz de un palito*
> *Y pedí a mi Dios clemente,*
> *Me perdonara el delito*
> *De haber muerto tanta gente.*
>
> . . . .
> *No sé si los recojeron,*
> *O si tal vez los caranchos*
> *Ay no más se los comieron.*

—*Ida*, IX

We are reminded[64] that in the romance of *Gualterio de Aquitania*, the hero did likewise after slaying his foes. This rite, I may say, seems quite objective. Martín knew that it was proper to perform it. But did he have a single pang? Or take the critical moment in the combat, just a few minutes before. He saw the first streak of dawn, and he hurriedly

---

62. *Vu*, XXI.
63. I piled together the corpses, knelt and prayed, made a little cross and begged my merciful God to forgive me for killing so many. . . I don't know if the bodies were taken up or if perhaps the vultures ate them on the spot.
64. Lugones, *Op. cit.*, 216.

promised the Virgin to be a very good man thenceforth if she would help him. If he was to save his skin before the full light came, it was time for prompt action. To me, the customary acts of crossing himself and praying to all the saints, before the onset, express more, and yet even they may not be more vital than the invocation of all the saints in Canto I, which call is surely an accepted epic convention. Perhaps the harshest religious criticism to be passed on this outcast man, is that the scant pious instruction he may ever have received, has stayed with him only in patches and tattered coverings. Circumstances bring it temporarily to his mind again. But in his response to nature, to human affection, and to certain ideals—not many, but some rather fine ones—there is the life of the spirit. The other personages seem like him in this respect. Theirs is the life of the vast open spaces: like most plainsmen and sailors, they are rough, and ready with their weapons, used to physical pain, brave but not devout. So we explain the fact that Martín intervened and killed the Indian who was torturing the white woman—standing by one of his own race. If you call him a "Christian soldier," put the stress very decidedly on "soldier." And do not fail to note his superstitions! They are numberless. They say there's an "evil light," as of an *âme en peine,* which hovers oft over the spot where is buried the negro Martín killed in the dance.[65] Fierro's son tied to Viscacha's hand a cowbell, at his dying hour, and weeping, witnessed the old rascal's shuffling off. A peon buried Viscacha, and, says Fierro, the next day they found one hand protruding from the grave![66] We can fairly see the horrid dreams, waking and sleeping, of the unhappy youth, whose brain is a nest of superstitions. (Read Canto XIX of *La Vuelta,* for a treasure of them!) Picardía charged the mulatto serving-wench with his failure to say correctly the articles of the creed. Witchcraft, certainly, but in this case very easily explained![67]

I have touched too frequently on the relations between man and man, to spend time here over the ethics of the poem. We have felt the presence of ideals. Men like Martín Fierro were loyal friends, kindly disposed, hospitable, affectionate fathers. Such men, if they kill duelling opponents, may feel remorse, but consider themselves justified by the rude code of gaucho chivalry. The two deaths Martín brings about in the duels narrated in *La Ida,* and his justification of them, such

---

65. *Ida,* VI.
66. *Vu,* XXI.
67. *Vu,* XVI.

as it is, in *Vu, XI*, are essential to the complete portrayal of this bizarre personality.

When the son of Cruz learns of his parentage, he forsakes cheating at cards as an occupation. Let such acts be opposed to the frailties which we do not seek to excuse. What remains with us, after studying the poem, is the conviction that the singer speaks for others as well as for himself: is doing a social service, and confidently foresees a better day for the land. It is in the assurance that this day shall be better morally as well as materially, that the ethical beauty of *Martín Fierro* resides.

VII

The Indians

I n its epic function of antagonist of the gauchos, the pampa is revealed as many-sided. It moulds with its myriad influences the gaucho life, as the sea fashions the sailor's. These influences are above, beneath, all around, in all the manifestations of nature, in all her kingdoms, notably the animal. What then, shall we not expect from that man whose home the entire pampa originally was?

Highly romantic, and yet awful, are the elements which the Indian in *Martín Fierro* brings to the concept of the desert. The following Cantos of *La Ida* refer to him: III, IV (one reference of little importance), V, VI, XII (by implication, when Cruz speaks of the shifting frontier and projects for its defense), XIII. In *La Vuelta*, Indian life is described in Cantos II–X, XI (Martín says he passed five years among the savages), XXV–XXVIII (but only by implication, in the references to frontier cantonments), and XXXII.[1] Eliminating these passing references and implications, the Indian section is narrowed down to Cantos III, V, and VI of *La Ida*, in which Fierro considers the Indians as his personal foes; XIII, the link between the two parts of the whole poem, in which Indianland is considered as a possible asylum for white outlaws; and Cantos II–X of *La Vuelta*. Here the minstrel sings of the Indians as a social unit fighting the white race, but nevertheless actually offering a precarious hospitality to individuals of that race. The individualistic point of view of Cantos III, V, and VI of *La Ida* harmonizes with the far greater plasticity, simplicity, vigor, and epic quality of this Part; while the leisurely Indian descriptions of the first third of *La Vuelta*, and the tendency to speak of everything *en bloc*, are in accord with the more didactic and generalizing style of Part II. The reader will have already inferred that to learn about the Indians, we turn to *La Vuelta;* to feel their menace, the constant factor of dread that they injected into the ranchman's life, we need the strophes of *La Ida*, hurrying as the hoofbeats of those wild pampa steeds.

---

1. Bien lo pasa hasta entre Pampas   Even 'mongst Indians one fares well
    El que respeta a la gente.   Who respects other people.

Martín goes to the frontier to fight Indians. Approximately, the frontier line started on the Atlantic coast, somewhere near Bahía Blanca, and ran northeast, perhaps at times very much so because of Indian invasions, to Olavarría, Quenehuin, Paz, Rivadavia and Lavalle, whence it continued almost due west, to lose itself among the lagoons south of Santa Fe Province. Beyond these its course was rather northwest into Córdoba. Very likely Martín performed his service, and crossed the frontier, at some point southwest of Olavarría, as we have seen elsewhere.[2]

It must not be thought for a moment that *Martín Fierro* offers much definite help in the disputed details of geography. To Gradgrind facts, the poet prefers a romantic vagueness, and those of his readers who know the field best, and might accordingly be expected to demand familiar facts, are the least disposed to complain of their absence.

The test of battle came more than a year after Martín arrived at the frontier garrison. This period before the storm is utilized to make us thoroughly aware of the clouds of threatened invasion. We see them lower in all their dreadfulness. For accompaniment, instead of peals of thunder, the beat of horses' hoofs and the devilish warcries of the Indians are described. And so Fierro is justified in saying, Let no man plead for the Indian, who robs and kills wherever he passes. Fiendish! we exclaim at some of the cruelties he alleges, but we of the North should easily be able to find their like in the story of our own pioneer days.

What is perhaps more novel is the consistent use of the place-name *pampas*, instead of any tribal name, such as *Araucanos, Ranqueles, Puelches*, and the like.[3]

The Indian invasion is called a *malón*. What a composite picture of border forays we have, if we supplement was to advance at a gallop lying close along the shoulder the story in *Ida*, III, with the accounts in Ascasubi, Echeverría and Leguizamón![4] The redskins' mode of attack and side of the horse,[5] until fairly near the enemy, and then swing into

---

2. References in *Ida*, III, and *Vu*, X; in the *Santos Vega* of Ascasubi; in Rojas' work (493N.); discussion with citizens of the Province of Buenos Aires; numerous passages in Mansilla's invaluable *Excuraión a los Indios Ranqueles;* and the *Descripción amena de la República Argentina* by E. S. Zeballos, especially the map accompanying Vol. II, lead to this conclusion.

3. Cf. *Manual de la Historia de la Civilización Argentina*, 123–153.

4. *Montaraz, passim.*

5. Leturque: *Au Pays des Gauchos*, 268.

the saddle, utter their warcry, and charge, whirling their cane lances. Not one thrust did they lose (*pues no hay lanzaso que pierde*).[6] Aside from the lance, the Indian used the *bolas,* already described. He had no firearms, but neither had his gaucho opponent, usually.

The South American Indian did not scalp, but the man he lanced was generally in a bad way, and Martín says he and the other conscripts ran like doves before hawks, in that day of their real testing. Several features of this thrilling encounter have now to be considered.

First, these Indians, like their Sioux cousins, did not loiter![7]

Second, and again like the North American Indians, they fought individually.[8]

Third, there was no quarter on either side. "Quarter!" said the Yankee frontiersman to his Indian foe, "I'll halve ye, and the devil may quarter ye!" Even so Martín tells us:[9]

> *Lo pise en las paletas,*
> *Yo hice la obra santa*
> *de hacerlo estirar la jeta.*
>
> —*Ida,* III

Verily, a tooth for a tooth!

Fourth, the Indians did not "carry on." They preferred to strike and run, even flee to avoid a disastrous combat, says Mansilla.[10]

I am aware that all these notes present the white man's viewpoint solely. As if Martín had an uneasy feeling that there was a side of humanity and mercy which should be heard when the "savages" were discussed, he made the remark cited above, about fair play among them.[11] But this is the white man and his uneasy conscience: Hernández does not attempt to speak from the standpoint of the hostile race, nor, so far as I know, does any Argentine voice valiantly and clearly plead

---

6. *Ida,* III.

7. *Como una luz de lijeros!*—*Ida,* III.

8. *Este quiero, este no quiero.*—*Ibid.*

9.   *I stamped on his shoulder-blades,*
                        I did the good job
                        Of making him croak!

10. *Op. cit.,* 305.

11. *Vu,* XXXII.

their cause today. What is most pathetic of all, the Indian does not speak for himself.

The whole protracted misery of border warfare was unnecessary, we learn in Canto V. Martín says his chiefs did not want to remedy the evil, and this defect makes him naturally the more contemptuous of those robbing Indians. Were they always robbers? In the attempt to answer this, we do not linger over their burning and pillaging invasions, in which they thought themselves completely justified, but we study their habits at home, as Fierro saw them. Apparently our answer is found in Canto IV of *La Vuelta*:[12]

> *De noche, les asiguro*
> *Para tenerlo seguro*
> *Le hace cerco la familia.*

Why? Not because they were unable to hobble the beast! Mansilla corroborates this charge of Fierro's.[13]

The old order changeth, even in Martín's unprogressive world, and a certain Don Ganza, Minister of War, plans to take the field against the Indians. That fixes the date of the action. Ganza was Minister for Sarmiento, in 1868, and the expedition to make a clean sweep of the savages, even to their remote villages, was doubtless planned soon after he entered upon his ministerial duties. Martín, however, is skeptical, probably because of many previous disillusions. "Those stratagems," he says, "don't take in foxes like me."[14] And the bad situation was to continue with only sporadic alleviations, until in the year 1875 Gen. Julio A. Roca subdued the Araucanians completely by doing what "Don Ganza" promised in our poem to do.

Canto XIII is transitional, as I said above, and so very properly Martín's frame of mind is seen to be changing. He is even able to say:[15]

12.
> *I assure you, that at night*
> *To keep him (i.e., the horse) safe*
> *The family sleeps surrounding him.*

13. *Op. cit.*, 391.
14. *Ida*, VI.
15.
> *There (i.e., with the Indians) will be safety*
> *And there will be great happiness.*

Allá harbrá siguridá
Y ha de haber grande alegría.

Later in the same Canto, however, he is none too sure of "the promised land," if we may infer from his tears. And when he returns to the land of the *ombú,* several years after, he knows better. Indianland will not serve for the white man.[16]

Pues infierno por infierno
Prefiero el de la frontera.

—*Vu,* X

Mansilla[17] reports similar experiences. But the transitional attitude of Canto XIII was vital to the argument of the poem, and its merit is higher for being so completely natural.

And so we come to the life of Fierro and Cruz among the braves: a chain of many well-wrought incidents, strung on the true gaucho cord of comment satiric or pathetic, but ever just and sensible. First we note an organized manifestation of this new life, in what I suppose we might call a parliamentary session. "Indians are great on speech-making" would be our present-day equivalent of Fierro's description of this noisy affair. There is something fine, in this picture of the pampa warriors who force their horses to make a wide circle, and listen, on horseback, for hours to the periods of some Araucanian Demosthenes: "Let us go and fight—the whites." Other parts of the machinery of government are duly mentioned: the *cacique,* for example, spares the lives of the two adventurers at the moment of their first entrance into the village, else—! His rule was hereditary, according to Mansilla, but the same authority quotes a powerful *cacique* to this effect: "Here, you've got to have an understanding first with the other chiefs, then with the captains, then the old men. All are free, all equal."[18]

In the long councils, the name of God was invoked.[19] The Araucanians' religion was elemental. Fierro does not tell us of their God, but does

---

16.   *Since, if it is a choice between two hells*
           I prefer that of the frontier.

17. *Op. cit., passim.*
18. *Ibid.,* 308.
19. *Ibid.,* 441.

introduce their devil, who is styled *gualicho*,[20] and is not so powerful as their God, according to Mansilla.[21] To withstand the wiles of this personage, the pampas rely on their *adivinas,* or female sooth-sayers.[22] If these fail, they are put to death. The awful means adopted by these hags to rid the village of the black pox, cause the same horror in us as in Fierro. A poor sufferer is smeared from head to foot with grease, and put out in the sun to boil![23] Hudson tells of methods equally barbarous, employed among the whites in those days.[24] When a hardy gaucho says of the remedies, "it is horrible to witness them," I feel sure that he is not over-stating the facts.

As to morality, thieving is not unknown, as we have read. Fierro piles up the indictment:[25]

> *El barbaro solo sabe*
> *Emborracharse y peliar.*
>
> —*Vu, IV*

And the voices of Echeverría, Leguizamón, Mansilla, and many another observer, in accord with the charge of Fierro, emphasize the shocking proportions of drunkenness then and now among the pampa Indians, as it has surely been the scourge of the North American tribes.

Cleanliness does not exist:[26]

> *Viven lo mesmo que el cerdo*
> *En esos toldos inmundos.*
>
> —*Vu, IV*

---

20. *Vu,* VI.
21. *Op. cit.,* 329 ff.
22. *Vu,* VI.
23. *Ibid.*
24. *El Ombú,* 63 ff.
25.   *The savage knows only*
            How to get drunk and fight.
26.   *They live like swine*
            In those filthy tents.

Mansilla, too, finds, amid general disgusting filthiness, only an occasional exception.[27]

The Indian is cruel in his treatment of his women. Cantos IX and X reveal incredible brutality in the domestic relations.

Prostitution and seduction are unknown, writes Mansilla.[28] In the same chapter he mentions three modes of marriage, all involving payment!

It will not be expected that abstractions appeal to such savages, and as a matter of fact, the ideas of conscience and honor are said to be non-existent among them. The dead are held in profound veneration, and at the grave of Cruz, Fierro passes long hours undisturbed.

In some, not very complex, ethical relations, Fierro occasionally found an Indian who excelled. Read this of their protector, the *cacique*:[29]

> *El que nos salvó al llegar*
> *Era el más hospitalario.*
> *Mostró noble corazon,*
> *Cristiano anhelaba ser—*
> *La justicia es un deber,*
> *Y sus méritos no callo,—*
> *Nos regaló unos caballos*
> *Y a veces nos vino a ver.*
>
> —*Vu*, VI

Frankness, generosity, hospitality: this is no common meed of praise! It prepares us for another commendatory strophe, in which the application is general.[30]

---

27. *Op. cit.*, 280, 357.
28. *Op. cit.*, 293.
29.
> *He who saved us when we came*
> *Was the most hospitable.*
> *He showed real nobility*
> *And was eager to be a Christian—*
> *One has to give others their due,*
> *And I want to praise his virtues,—*
> *He gave us a few horses*
> *And visited us at times.*

30.
> *They divide the spoil*
> *Justly, honorably;*
> *The Indian displays no greed—*
> *Commits no wrong.*

Se reparten el botín
Con igualdá, sin malicia;
No muestra el indio codicia
Ninguna falta comete
Solo en esto se somete
A una regla de justicia.

—*Vu,* V

The *modus vivendi* in the villages was, briefly, as among the North American redskins: the women worked, the braves loafed or hunted.[31] The Indian sometimes obtained liquor and then he became a loathsome beast.[32] Another repulsive custom was that of drinking the blood of slaughtered animals.[33] The Indian diet was well-nigh restricted to meat, much of the time. At intervals the savory *mazamorra* and many other dishes, described in Chapter VI, appeared in the Indian's tent. Like so many wolves, the inmates devoured them, and scant indeed were the scraps which remained to be thrown to the domestic animals.[34]

However, the treatment of the horse is an exception to this general rule. Excellent care is taken of him. In Canto IV of *La Vuelta,* Martín displays the keenest interest in Indian horses, while Canto X is nothing short of a rhapsody on them and the Indians' care and training of them. Incidentally it is a sharp criticism of some gaucho methods of treating the animal.

While among the Indians, Martín did not notice closely the details of the feminine wardrobe. "Ragged," he styles the women in Canto V. The braves are said to undertake an invasion half-naked.[35] If they were ever more abundantly clothed, the luxury was due, either to good luck in the invasion, or to chaffering with merchants on the Chilean or Argentine border. In Cantos IV and V we find the word *prendas,* which here signifies ornaments, often of silver. The *Manual de Historia de la*

In this act alone, he submits
To a principle of right.

31. *Vu,* III, IV.
32. Mansilla: *Op. cit., passim.*
33. *Vu,* II.
34. *Vu,* VII.
35. *Vu,* IV.

Civilización Argentina[36] supplies some details of dress: cloaks of sewn skins, woolen ponchos, leather boots.[36a]

The *toldos* or tents in which the Indians lived were constructed of *horcones* or posts arranged to form the outline of a square, and covered with hides.[37]

To prove that life was not Arcadian, the story of the Christian captive in Canto VIII of *La Vuelta* would suffice. A *cacique* might have several wives. It was all a question of means. The Indian of Canto VII had introduced this captive woman among his other "squaws." The inevitable jealousies followed, until at last a jilted *china* accused the Christian captive of witchcraft.

Martín vouches for a curious practice, related to the physical characteristics of the savages. The mother flattened the back of her baby's head by binding it to a board. This practice is known among the Indians of our Northwest. Also, a pointed skull was highly esteemed, as it was by the Aztecs.[38] He says never a word about height or muscular development, or about feminine physique. But he does emphasize the toughness of the Indian,[39] and his strength may be inferred from such lines as:[40]

> *Si lo alcanza, sin vida*
> *Es seguro que lo deja.*
>
> —*Ibid*

In the *Manual* referred to, we find the Araucanians to be of middle height, if not short, having aquiline noses, short hair, and a generally excellent muscular development.[41]

My earlier conjecture as to the number of warriors in the tribe when Cruz and Fierro came to it, placed the figure at a possible two hundred. But after reading Mansilla's invaluable work, this conjecture seems

---

36. 126.

36. The illustrations in this work, in that of Rojas, and in the *Excursión* of Mansilla, are all excellent sources of information.

37. *Ibid.*, 127.

38. *Vu*, VIII.

39. *Ida*, III.

40.   *If he hits you (with the* bolas*)*
                           He'll surely leave you a corpse.

41. 148.

unduly large. Evidently the tribes numbered their hundreds rather than thousands. Their interrelations being very variable, they might, for an invasion, muster, with their neighbors, a large company. In the great foray described by Santos Vega five thousand Indians took the field,[42] but this was long before Fierro's epoch, and Hernández tells us:[43]

Las tribus estan deshechas,

. . . .

Y de la chusma y la lanza
Ya quedan muy pocos vivos.

—*Vu*, V

The language of the pampa Indians and the vocabularies they have given to Spanish really constitute a theme of absorbing interest for the philologist, but must be summarily treated in this work. *Martín Fierro* does not afford much direct philological assistance. It is, however, rich in Kechuan and Guaraní terms.[44]

---

42. Ascasubi's *Santos Vega*, 226.

43.   *The tribes are broken up,*

                      . . . .
                 And very few remain alive
                    Of the rank and file
                  Who once wielded lance.

44. The Spanish phrases used by Indians in *Martín Fierro* are, as they are grotesquely recast by gaucho lips:

Acabau cristiano—Metau el lanza hasta el pluma.—*Ida*, III—(I'll end this Christian!—I'll stick my lance in him, up to the plume!)

Huainca!—*Vu*, II—(I.e., a person not an Indian.)

Ioká-ioká!—*Vu*, V—(Apparently, a ritualistic term, whose meaning I cannot find.)

Crístiano echando gualicho.—*Vu*, VI—(The Christian's throwing an evil spell.)

Confechando no querés.—*Vu*, VIII—(You won't confess?)

Scant as the mutilated Spanish is, one may deduce from it:

First, that the Araucanians, when they expressed themselves in Spanish, had a tendency to cast their verb forms in the mold of the first conjugation, e.g., *metau* for *metado* instead of *metido*.

Second, that there is frequent confusion of genders, *e.g., el lanza.*

Third, that the participle and gerund are overworked:

metau, past participle, for the future indicative.

confechando, for the present infinitive.

Fourth, that there are elliptical expressions. All four of the characteristics observed seem quite normal in the case of savages who try to express themselves in a highly developed language, and whose attempt is reported to us secondhand.

Although the Araucanian did not contribute so much, quantitatively speaking, to Spanish as either the Kechuan or the Guaraní, nevertheless its quota is not without value. Rojas calls attention to the fact that it was with the *pampa* Indians, on the plains of Buenos Aires Province, that our minstrels had the most frequent contacts, and consequently their greatest incentives to composition on Indian themes, must have been received from these Araucanians.[45]

To return to the vocabulary, the Araucanian tongue furnishes Argentine geography with many proper names, e.g., Leubucó, Quenque, Carrilauquén, Codihué; and daily life with some of the commonest words, such as: *laucha* (mouse), *guasca* (thong), *chicha* (an alcoholic drink), *chiripá, choclo* (corn), *chuño* (flour from potato or corn), *chakra* (small farm), *chala* (leaf of maize), etc.[46] A greater objectivity and a certain picturesque-tongue is none other than Araucanian, as it is spoken east of the Andes. ness in speech, are secured by the Araucanian words on Martín's tongue.

It is a fairly well developed and not very difficult tongue. The pronunciation must have seemed *gangoso,* or thick and slovenly, even to the gauchos who were half Indians. Fierro's foe, in *Vu,* VIII, cries, *confechando* instead of *confesando.* Sometimes the tongue was "twisted sidewise," says Febrés![47] Nevertheless, loud speaking was possible, as when in the "parliament," the demoniacal yells arose at any provocation or at none.[48] Febrés says, too, that before pauses, the speaker would both raise his voice and prolong the note.[49]

Specimens of Araucanian poetry, sacred and profane, are found in Rojas.[50] The characteristically sombre tone and the primitive ritualism (of which the "parliament" of *Vu,* II, represents, according to this author, the "Nguillatum" or a very like ceremony), betoken a race of children, swayed by the first rude religious instincts of mankind.

We are now confronted by these questions:

Is Fierro, as a typical gaucho, conscious of his Indian ancestry?

What did he inherit from Indian forbears?

---

45. *Op. cit.,* 122.

46. Cf. Andrés Febrés: *Gramática Araucana,* Introd., vii: The pampa tongue is none other than Araucanian, as it is spoken east of the Andes.

47. *Ibid.*

48. *Vu,* II.

49. *Op. cit.,* 37.

50. *Op. cit.,* 112–116.

What do the Indians mean to him in Argentina's drama of national expansion, in which he himself is an actor?

To the first question, an unqualifiedly negative answer must be given. Were there any consciousness of kinship with the Indian, somewhere in the poem we should have its expression. Martín praises the Indians' skill, and of his own volition seeks an asylum with them, but blood ties do not exist for him. It is one thing to receive fraternal treatment, such as the *cacique* who spared Martín's life gave him; it is quite another thing to feel and acknowledge oneself a brother to the benefactor.

Nevertheless, Fierro inherited various Indian qualities. His savage ancestors, if we accept the *mestización* theory for his case, had given him straight hair, prominent features, and a skin of bronze. To his patrimony as the son of ruthless Spanish warriors, was added the wild natural need of the great plains, of the cattle, of the open air and the nomadic existence. Superstitions too were not lacking.[51] Many traces appear in the course of our poem.[52] But these beliefs did not reign unrivalled in Martín's spirit. His Spanish great-grandfather bequeathed to him, together with a frame of iron, an instinctive, illogical loyalty to Christianity in the Roman form.

Indian ancestors gave the gaucho his keen vision, the hunter's agility, astuteness, and persistence, familiarity with all species of animals, and ability to use the *bolas*.[53] It may be objected that none of these qualities is the exclusive possession of the savage, but one may at least affirm that they were displayed in their fullest glory among the Indians. Martín admits it, as though recognizing his teachers in the savages.[54]

Sabe manejar las bolas
Como naides las maneja.

—*Ida*, III

---

51. For some of them, Ambrosetti's valuable *Supersticiones y Leyendas* may be consulted, especially the second half.
52. Cf. Chapt. VI.
53. While Mrtín copies the red men in the use of the *bolas,* his mode of fighting shows no slavish imitation. His weapons and equipment are generally superior.
54.   *He can use the* bolas
                As no one else can.

Tiene la vista del águila,
Del león la temeridá—
En el desierto no habrá
Animal que él no lo entienda.[55]

—*Vu,* IV

Tracker's and trapper's skill was also bequeathed by the Indians.[56] Some universally worn articles of clothing, as the *poncho,* and the *chiripá,* are of Indian origin.

It were useless to deny that the Indian words of which we have spoken, and which entered into the daily life of the plainsman, were a part of Fierro's intellectual inheritance. But I cannot believe that the purely Indian concepts affected Fierro's thinking to any great degree.

Codes of honor, social customs and sanctions, were given the gaucho by his Spanish fathers.

The Indian as an actor in the national drama, added another element of dread to the "desert" concept. Because he was a foe, he was constantly proving the Christian's mettle. As cold weather has stimulated the races of the temperate zones, so the Indian peril kept the gauchos alert, under arms, accustomed to the toils and perils of war.[57] The eternal opposition of Christianity and paganism was ever present to the gaucho's mind.[58] Shall we not conclude that in the unending strife a certain code of frontier chivalry was developed, or at least stimulated among the gauchos, just as the frontier wars with the Moors for so many centuries developed the Spanish chivalry?

It is therefore not strange that Fierro leaped to the captive's defense, and that he treated her with pity. He would have understood the spirit of Henry IV's

> *"Down, down with every foreigner,*
> *But let your brethren go!"*

55.
> *He has the eagle's vision,*
> *The lion's boldness,*
> *There'll not be in the pampa*
> *An animal he doesn't know all about.*

56. *Vu,* IV.
57. *Ida,* III.
58. *Vu, passim.*

But the red men were an inspiration also in some of the activities of peace. I have called attention to their superiority to the gauchos in "bronco-busting," and the art of following a trail is beautifully pictured by their pupil, in Canto X of *La Vuelta*. Sad to relate, once the pupils learned these lessons, they turned again and rent their teachers. We read the same in our North American history. The red men had lived out their hour, and were doomed to fade into oblivion, with this for consolation, had they but discerned the signs of the times, that their bitterest foes, the gauchos of the pampa, were hastening to fulfil the same mournful, inexorable destiny.

VIII

The Literary Value of "Martín Fierro"

The two Parts of *Martín Fierro* present a variety of literary forms. *La Ida* is practically all epic material. Likewise, in *La Vuelta*, the first ten cantos may be conveniently accepted *en bloc* as epic, for even where the single lines do not justify the use of this term, as for instance the elegiac strains at the death of Cruz, the underlying principle exists always. Cantos XI and XII of *La Vuelta* may be regarded as a not specially inspired but quite necessary appendix to the chief epic portion.

In Canto XX appears a new personage, Picardía, who is later discovered to be the son of Cruz. His adventures are those of a full-sized *pícaro*, but like the hero of the great Spanish picaresque novel *Lazarillo de Tormes*, he was not born so. Taking into consideration the expansiveness of his schemes of deception, intrigue, and brutality, ranging all the way from the individual to the universal; the broad interests, actual as well as potential, which are involved; and the vastness of the poetic stage—all this, on the one hand, and on the other the fact that Picardía reveals himself to be the son of Cruz—we are clearly conscious of an epic flavor in Cantos XX–XXVIII, and a more than casual relation to the epic of Part I. Canto XXXI is a transitional narrative, and Canto XXX contains that precious episode, the already described *payada de contrapunto* between the negro and Fierro. It is a lyric gem in an epic setting. It cannot be dissociated from the stress and strain of the hero's life in Part I. Says Martín:[1]

> *Aura son estos morenos*
> *Pa alivio de mi vejez. . .*
> *Pero firme en mi destino*
> *Hasta el fin he de seguir.*
>
> *—Vu, XXX*

---

1. *Now these black men*
Are to console my old age. . .
But firm in the strength of my destiny
I follow on to the finish.

HENRY A. HOLMES AND JOSÉ HERNÁNDEZ

The objection may be raised, that this analysis omits, in both parts, certain cantos which for the sake of consistency ought to be included in the epic section. These cantos, moreover, are intimately connected with the main characters and threads of the story. I admit the force of this objection, and should be rather pleased than otherwise to hear it advanced, for I have felt at times a keen inclination to place the cantos in question on a par with those sections classed as particularly epic; and have been forced to conclude that it is impossible, in any canto of the entire poem, to get wholly away from the atmosphere of the epic. But in *La Ida,* I note in Canto VI the elegy on "the abandoned home;" in IV, V, and XII, satiric verse; in IX, some purest lyric—in fact, two entire pages of it form a piquant contrast to the fight that follows.

Cantos XIII–XIX of *La Vuelta,* narrate young Fierro's life with an old rascal named Viscacha. The latter reminds us strongly of one of Espronceda's characters, the old convict in *El Diablo Mundo* who gave such picturesque advice to Fabio. These cantos are epic "asides;" they are a set of little novels or impressions done in quick glaring colors. The cynical satire of Viscacha is unforgettable. He pillories well-nigh all mankind.

It were well, also, not to overlook the very palpable dramatic tendency in Cantos XXIV and XXV. We may assume that in this section Picardía impersonated freely the characters of whom he was singing.

Cantos XXXI–XXXIII are mainly didactic. Martín gives fatherly advice to his sons and Picardía. The poet, too, has his little word. The epic thrills of the earlier cantos having subsided, action gives place to moralizing, and the poem closes on a serious but not exalted or dramatic plane. Retrospective calm follows the former agonizing struggles of Fierro, as a peaceful sunset may succeed a storm-racked day. But the veiled threat of the negro must not be overlooked.[2] Other stoms may arise. Fierro's antagonists may come again to grips with him, for all his change of name (XXXIII). An observation of Gummere[3] applies to this truly epic feature: "primitive ballads, however inadequate they would seem for our own needs, come from men who knew life at its hardest,

---

2. In this connection, read the apparently remorseful admission of Martín to his sons in *Vu,* XXXII, concerning the killing of the negro at the ball. These three strophes (particularly when we remember what Martín had previously said, in *Vu,* XI), do much to heighten the relief of the entire poem of *Martín Fierro.*
3. *The Popular Ballads,* 343.

faced it, accepted it, well aware that a losing fight is at the end of every march."

The vast majority of the strophes in both *La Ida* and *La Vuelta* show the following rhyme sequence, which is used for all purposes, elegy, narration, satire, lyric:

—A
—B
—B
—C
—C
—B

It is understood that this scheme refers to individual strophes merely. The rhymes themselves vary from stanza to stanza. In both Part I and Part II, the first canto, and most of the following cantos, begin with this arrangement, which is employed two hundred and seventy-eight times in *La Ida* and six hundred and thirty-two in *La Vuelta*. Without reckoning sporadic verse-combinations differing from the above, we find in *Martín Fierro* three other sequences interspersed, with consequent prevention of monotony.

The first and most frequent of these alternations runs thus:

—A
—B
—B
—C
—B
—C

This too is used in narration and in all the other poetic types. There seems to be no other reason for its introduction than the desire to avoid monotony. In *La Ida*, sixty-eight strophes of this class are found; in *La Vuelta*, sixty-seven. But *La Vuelta* is more than twice as long as *La Ida*.

Cuartetas are employed rather more often in Part II than in Part I; Cf. *Ida*, VII and VIII, and *Vu*, XXVII and XXVIII. Here narrative predominates, though with an occasional satiric or elegiac touch.

The third variant is the *romance* form, occurring in Cantos XI, XX, XXIX, and XXXI of *La Vuelta*.

Hernández seems to value it chiefly for interludes or transitional passages. Thus in *Vu*, XI, Fierro, after ending his own story, introduces his sons; in XX, appears Picardía; in XXIX, the negro, and in XXXI, the company breaks up after the *payada*, and we are prepared for Fierro's last verses of counsel. These short *romances* are at once interludes and introductions.

Hernández is expert in their use, but no less so in that of the six-verse combination previously examined. Whence came this unusual form? We recall the *décimas* cited in Chapter II, and how the *décimas* as a form, together with the *romance,* all contributed something to the development of popular poetry, a poetry which was capable of being bent to this use or that, as time and temperament might demand. The *décima* might, then, in the course of time, fulfil not merely a lyric, but also an epic purpose. Examination shows that the last six verses of a *décima*, taken by themselves, yield the very structure we have found prevalent in *Hernández.* For corroboration, I cite the following from Rojas: "In the *décima* is included the. . . six-verse strophe which *José* Hernández preferred for composing *Martín Fierro.*"[4]

Again, in the tribute from Unamuno which is quoted at the close of this chapter, the verse structure is referred to as the *décima.* It is found also in *Los Tres Gauchos Orientales y el Matrero Luciano Santos* of Lussich.[5] Who decapitated the integral *décima* to gain the form under discussion, we cannot say. But there the result stands—a highly successful one in the case of Hernández. The verses are not allowed to forget their pristine lyric function, in working out a generally epic purpose. In fact, their effectiveness is surprising.

Many of the verses thrill with music. One of the commonplaces which the reader is apt to forget, is that the entire poem is, theoretically, to be sung. In *Ida*, VII and VIII, the singer passes from one form to another, as varying moods possess him, and in *Ida,* XI, to enhance the grace of that famous gaucho dance, the *pericón, seguidillas* are sung by the guitarrist:[6]

> *Las mujeres son todas*
> *Como las mulas, etc.*

---

4. *Op. cit.,* 216. He terms it a *sextina.* He says the *payadores* preferred to it either *coplas* or the *romance.*
5. Cf. Lugones, *op. cit.,* 189.
6.   *Women are all—Like mules.*

Were we to ignore the "elegant voluptuousness" of the dance which gives occasion to these verses, we should be at a loss to account for their presence. Songs were a feature of the old gaucho *pericón,* says Rojas,[7] and the *payadores* often introduced lyric novelties.

The value of the lyric form in *Martín Fierro* is precisely that it aids in maintaining fresh the heritage of all the old *payadores,* of whom Fierro is a specimen and Santos Vega the archetype. Had Hernández chosen another form for his defense of the gauchos—had he cast it, for instance, in the mold of *La Araucana*—it would not have been in keeping with either the theme or the setting. We have seen elsewhere how the gauchos sang at work or play, in love and in war. Our author keeps faith with their nature, using their music as well as their speech, and the epic qualities in his subject make an impressive narration inevitable, despite the guitar and the popular meter.

The custom of the gaucho singer is to prolong indefinitely the ultimate syllable of the verse. It has been suggested that this curiously mournful prolongation is inherited from old Spain, and that perhaps the church hymns, with their many accented *últimas,* are particularly responsible for this.[8]

Let us now consider the gaucho vocabulary with regard to its literary function.[9] In its use, Hernández is quite consistent. Few of his verses fail to spring directly from the gauchos' own lips. Mitre criticised him for this.[10] In his *Armonías,* Mitre could have made use of the same racy language, but he believed that a sense of art proscribed it. The results speak for themselves. We are not thrilled by Mitre—nor indeed by Echeverría—and we *are* thrilled by Hernández, who lost conciousness of himself in his heroes. One does not object to the occasional roughness of the *Cantar del Cid.* Shakespeare and Cervantes are now and then "vulgar", that is, true to life. The gaucho manner of speech is one of the chief components of the local color, one which Hernández felt deeply and used effectively. Such employment is an art. And regarding the use of local color, it is here in place to state the following thesis, which may be found in slightly different form in Rojas:[11] *Martín Fierro* does not abound in narrowly specific details, because it is dealing with universals

---

7. *Op. cit.,* 238.
8. Cf. Menéndez y Pelayo, *Antología de Poetas Líricos Castellanos,* XI, 124–125.
9. Cf. the note on the gaucho language in Chapter VI.
10. Cf. letter of thanks for presentation copy, in the Introduction to the Edition of 1894.
11. *Op. cit.,* 295.

on an epic canvas. You may place the hero's rancho at Pergamino or at Dolores: the essential elements of gaucho life are the same. And it was these elements, faithfully and sympathetically reproduced, which assured for the poem an instantaneous success. The *rancho,* the *fogón* (or fireside), the rough, hearty dishes prepared by the *china,* the gaucho's horse and his outfit, his life, his pleasures, his service and suffering: all these things you may have on your lips and in your heart, if you will read *Martín Fierro.* It is a gaucho dictionary; or shall we say, the gaucho's Bible?

Rojas, who has so admirably studied *Martín Fierro,* showing that scholarship need not suffer while a tribute of grateful admiration is being rendered, has said that the gaucho epoch in Argentine literature produced two epics: *Martín Fierro* in verse and *Facundo* in prose. *Facundo* is by Domingo F. Sarmiento. It was first published in 1845 with the title: *Facundo, o La Civilización y la Barbarie.* It is a polemic, like Hernández' poem, but, oddly enough, it is essentially *against* the gaucho's unprogressiveness and degradation, with barbarism as a resultant. The first part of *Facundo* is a vivid picture of the pampa, the gaucho, and his life. Willy nilly, Sarmiento pictures these with great spirit. In Part II, while seeming to flay Facundo Quiroga, a provincial gaucho chief, he is actually showing up with tremendous effect that supreme gaucho tyrant, Rosas. And this book must be considered among the most potent forces contributing to Rosas' downfall in 1852. Politically and sociologically, Sarmiento made some mistakes in it, but he is so brilliant and impassioned a "special pleader," that one admires *Facundo* in spite of oneself. Since, however, its plan is open to serious criticism, and its style is of the every-day sort, journalistic, rather than universal, we must adjudge *Martín Fierro* more artistic in form and more general in appeal. Moreover, *Martín Fierro* is of, for, and by the gauchos.

For those who demand proof that it is artistic and universal, the following paragraphs are submitted.

Burdensome description is lacking. This is true of the Bible, of Homer, of Shakespeare. The reader will recall Homer's descriptive tag, "swift-footed," "loud-sounding," and the like, whose value we do not need to discuss. I cull at random from *Martín Fierro: en mi moro ensarciando* (on my mane-tossing black horse),[12] *el de ollín* (soot-faced negro),[13] *peligrosa*

---

12. *Ida,* III.
13. *Ida,* VI.

inquietud (dread born of threatening dangers),[14] *la tierra en donde crece el ombú* (the land of the *ombú*)[14]—what a host of associations this carries!—*un güey corneta* (troublesome steer or person).[15] The conclusion will be that in regard to terse, epigrammatic characterization, Hernández is a true follower of Homer. Surely one forceful, luminous phrase of Hernández is worth all the disquisitions of Sarmiento. Give us Fierro, one gaucho, at the ruins of his one and only home, with all his family scattered, and we can visualize a thousand gauchos in like evil case.

The hand that pens the slightly coarse epithet, the rude phrase not meant for the drawingroom, can in the next instant give us so emotional a verse as this:[16]

> *Por suerte en aquel momento*
> *Venía coloriando el alba, etc.*

Bear in mind that this Hector of horsemen has just been hewing and stabbing, and then—he catches a glimpse of dawn off in the east! He is transformed, and he invokes the Virgin as his protectress in the fearful battle with these cruel pursuers. There is a rich psychology in this passage: "By good luck. . . at that instant—The dawn came lighting up the sky." Wordsworth's was a strong emotion as he cried: "My heart leaps up when I behold a rainbow," but he is more wordy. The charm of Hernández' verse is to feel, as the gaucho feels, deeply but silently. His is in general a noble style.

Also, the poem is a poem of realities. How can a poem claim to be epic and deal with any other realm than that of realities? "I sing of arms"—true, oh Virgil! and Fierro too sings of arms, and of horses, of vast lands for chasing and racing, and of fiendish enemies to fight. 'Tis all primitive, and rude, and popular, and (possibly) brutal, but epics are frequently so, for they deal with very rough and apparently formless masses, through which darts a living flame, that spurs men on to action!

Likewise—and more especially is this true in the more decidedly epic portions—*Martín Fierro* is rapid in its movement. I challenge the reader not to be caught swaying in his chair in an inescapable participation, as he sees Fierro in the *mêlée* of Indians and conscripts.

---

14. *Vu*, X.
15. *Vu*, XVI.
16. *Ida*, IX.

One asks oneself how the action can be so rapid if the verse used in that description is the usual octosyllabic. Well, to appreciate the happy selection of the details is to give the answer. The ground trembles—Fierro's mount is slow—they flee like doves from hawks.[17] Vivid is the present tense in *si no traigo bolas*,[18] and *si me alcanza*,[19] etc. Under the hands of genius we see the theme bursting all the hampering bonds of the rhetoricians and hurtling along with such speed as that which ever and anon stirs us in the *Poema del mío Cid*.

Another quality is directness. There is no complicated intrigue. Tremendous, undeviating gallops across-country were a daily habit. Gauchos followed their leader, not his politics. Their platform, slogans, principles, were all direct. So is the story. The great primitive epics are shining examples of directness. There must be no tricks: bedazzlement and uncertainty do not become the epic. So Fierro's fellows speak out "straight." If Martín will be an outlaw, he resolves to be worse than a wild animal.[20] Throughout the work, one observes that a salient feature is the inexorable progress. When, in Picardía's story, the *Comandante* levies recruits for the frontier, the faces of the hapless victims flit by as do faces in the cinematograph.[21] Direct progress; direct speech. Ready epithets are hurled by the official at each man, and he is gone, without argument or irrelevant observations.

Some admirers of so stirring a narrative are inclined to wish that it had been made, as it were, an out-and-out epic: that all the pure lyric, and satirical, and didactic portions, had been excised. "Would not the essence of Part I," they say, "together with the first cantos of *La Vuelta* and the central thought of the Picardía story, constitute a fine, foursquare, pampa epic?" Yes—and no. A certain consistency might be attained, but at the expense of the poem's humanity. Let us remember the words of Victor Hugo: *Il y a tout dans tout*.[22] The instantaneous popular response to the criticised portions is their permanent justification. We may well believe that the writer whose heart was so aflame over gaucho wrongs, was the only writer who could thrill us with the *gesta* of the gauchos. Surely *Paradise Lost* is didactic, and the *Divine Comedy* is a

---

17. *Ida*, III.
18. Lit. "if I don't carry the *bolas*," i.e., had I lacked this weapon.
19. If he *gets* me.
20. *Ida*, VI.
21. *Vu*, XXV.
22. Preface to *Cromwell*.

series of fearsome fustigations. Let *Martín Fierro* follow these, if it be only from afar.

Of course to say the foregoing is to say that *Martín Fierro* is not a primitive or popular epic. That, at least, should be immediately apparent. For though Hernández really lost himself amazingly in the ensemble of his gauchos, nevertheless he was "there," and we know it. Every earnest plea for his protégés makes it more apparent. There remains one classification, and one alone, for *Martín Fierro*.

It is a popularized narration, epic in spirit, and epic in most essentials, but generally lyric in verse-form.

Voltaire says an epic is a recital in verse of heroic adventures.[23] *Martín Fierro* fulfils this condition, if in no other passage than the narrative of the crossing of the perilous desert. Martín is a hero, for, as representative, he defends as best he can, the inherent liberties of his *pago* (district), class, and race. That he is only a pawn in the game, does not deter him. He is great, because he has a great ideal, viz., refusal, in the name of liberty, to submit. He is the Argentine Robin Hood.[24]

"The marvellous" should be in the heart of the epic hero, says Larousse.[25] In Chapters I and VI, we have looked into the gaucho's heart. What did we find there if not lively imagination, profound superstitions, intimate communion with nature, and a vast capacity for heroism and suffering?

"To have an epic character, an event must bear the stamp of the absolute," pronounces the *Diccionario Hispano-Americano*. The disappearance of the gaucho,

---

23. Preface to *La Henriade*.

24. A phrase or two from the article on Robin Hood in the *Encyclopedia Britannica* (Edition XI, Vol. 23) will aid us to comprehend what the Argentine outlaws were and were not.

"The immediate genesis of the myth may well be sought in the *heartless* forest *laws*." (Omit the word "forest," and insert in its place: "administration of Argentine.")

"Robin Hood is the people's ideal, about the close of the middle ages. He readjusts the distribution of property. (Cf. what Fierro proposes in Canto XXXIII of *La Vuelta*: "The gaucho ought to have a home, schools, churches, and rights.") . . . He endows the poor. He is an earnest worshipper of the Virgin. . . He is the incomparable archer, the lover of the greenwood (English equivalent, in outlawry, of the pampa), and the free life, brave, adventurous, open-handed, a protector of women."

Some Argentine critic might have written most of this of Fierro's case! It is easy, after reading such a delineation, to understand why the Argentine peasants had to help the pampa outlaws—feed, house, entertain and conceal them.

25. *Dictionnaire:* articles on *The Epic*.

"When for a moment, like a drop of rain,
He sinks into the yeast of"

social waves, is fated, absolutely.

I mentioned Voltaire. In that same definition, the author of *La Henriade* allows the broadest possible scope to the action. But amplitude inheres in the epic, by or without the grace of Voltaire. Addison[26] said that Aristotle's rules for the epic cannot be supposed to quadrate exactly with the heroic poems written since his time. In other words, besides ample scope, the genre has demanded and will continue to demand, the right to evolve.

Surely enough has been said to confirm our poem in the right to be exactly what it is: not an anonymous work, but very successfully popularized, with stirring epic characteristics, in a lyric dress. If one wishes to call it a drama, we admit that it has its dramatic features. Its elegiac and satirical qualities have been remarked upon. The book teems with humor, now broad, now sly. Many of the popular sayings, which we noted in Chapter VI, abound in humor. And humor, as Ker observes,[27] is inseparable from all large fiction. Compare the broad humor of the French *chansons de geste*. Compare the episode of the chests in the *Poema del Cid*. "Ulysses is as old as Achilles."

What gives the essential unity to *Martín Fierro?* It is the collective picture of the gauchos, with all the value of their joys, sorrows, and gloomy destiny. It is the intense feeling which sees in the action something general, something abiding, for, as we are presently to observe, the gaucho still abides in spirit in Argentina. It is the powerfully direct influence of the desert.

As used in *Martín Fierro*, the desert has an extraordinarily epic value. A struggle is on, unfinished even in this year of grace 1922, a Titanic struggle between two eternal foes: Man and Nature. Roca conquered the Indians, and progress has eliminated many of the wrongs done the gaucho by commandant or store-keeper; but the unconquered foe, that sheltered the redskin and—we were on the point of saying—justified those oppressors, was and is *Nature*. She had her moods of charm, in which she grappled the gaucho to her with hoops

---

26. Quoted by Myers: *A Study in Epic Development*, 26.
27. *Epic and Romance*, 312.

of steel in an undying relationship.[28] She had, and still has, also, her savage, destructive side, her mysteries, her impenetrable reserves.[29] As Russia conquered Napoleon by her snows, so the desert has held out against the Argentines for so long, by a resistance perhaps the more awful because largely passive. During the age-long strife there have been superimposed yet other fatalistic elements upon the already superstitious, impressionable character which the Spanish pioneers brought to the land. The peculiar *señas*, the wicked smile and biting jest, the unutterably mournful cadences of the *tristes, vidalitas*, and other songs, the stormy sports, and chiefest of all, the features and garb of the gaucho, bear witness to this antagonism. Nor did the gaucho feel that only the Indians and the government were the ministers of his foe. In significant volume even then, and torrentially in later years, the tide of immigration beat upon him, scouring away the richness of the land and leaving only barrenness to its own sons. Complaints of this are numerous in *Martín Fierro*.[30] Small wonder that the robust heart of Hernández swelled over such wrongs.

---

28. Witness the following:

> The sun was disappearing for good. A broad livid belt stained the horizon and with its light, purple, changeful, splendid, gilded the piled-up western clouds, which, like shifting, snowy mountains, pierced the heaven in immense spirals and shapeless figures of immeasurable size. Aquilon the dry was furling his wings; gently, gayly, soft breezes cooled the traveller's brow; the grass billowed like the storm-vexed sea; sylvan flowers on slender stems painted the fields with brilliant hues; perfumes most mild, like the vague memory of love's first kiss, were borne on the intoxicating airs.
>
> The last rays of the sun wrapped the earth in their poetic, dusky mantle; daylight, dying amid night's mystic shadows, made way for the mistress of the heavens.
>
> The moon was already blazing among shimmering stars, when we came to the shores of a small lake, above whose crystal mirror numberless waterfowl were chanting in chorus. We halted—eased horses—and yearning for rest, I stretched myself on the soft grass, pillowing my head on my crossed arms.
>
> —Mansilla, *Op. cit.*, 462

29. Witness these lines:

> The hurricane roared, breaking down the trees; at short intervals electric currents pierced the dark vault of the heavens; the lightning twisted: up and down, sidewise, in straight lines and oblique, revealing, through the massed blackness, far-off stars; the hoarse thunder shook the air incessantly and our souls shrank within themselves, in the presence of imminent peril.
>
> —Mansilla, *Op. cit.*, 520

30. Cf. *Ida*, IV, V, and XII; *Vu*, XXIII: a peddling Neapolitan (*un napoles mercachifle*).

And yet there were redeeming aspects to this governmental rigor, this foreign invasion, which Fierro and his friends could not see. No one wishes to justify the baseless cruelty of an individual, but it is quite probable that as a social unit, the "government" was in straits as well as the peasants. The desert menaced those in power as well as those under authority. They must win or die—politically—and well they saw that with their political death would perish also certain immediate economic hopes. These dreams of development, frankly and naturally for personal profit mostly, but tightly bound up with the progress of the republic, did not elicit much sympathy from the gauchos. They were by inheritance very nearsighted in matters economic. When, therefore, the powers that were callously threw them as pawns into the strife, when they were brought into ruinous contact with industrious *gringos*,[31] with the Indians, and with Nature, all they felt was the tyranny of the act. The march of mankind is grandiose when measured by centuries. This the plainsmen failed to realize. Changing the figure, we may say that Fierro felt only the birth-pangs of the greater Argentina, without seeing how inevitable was that birth!

Thus the Pampa created the gauchos and also many of their tyrants, gave them her own strange education, and finally, like those other Titans Cronus and Rhea, challenged them to combat for the mastery. This combat, I repeat, has not yet been ended, though the poor Indian long since left the field. These handgrips with the colossal foe thrill every Argentine heart, and determine the foreign conception of Argentina. Hence, if the critics are looking for a fight, *Martín Fierro* supplies it, and not a one-man fight, but that of a whole society, a whole nation. On the one side, the gauchos; on the other, Nature and her minions. These are, besides natural phenomena, the Indians and the prosperous, governing class. I include the latter, because, as we have seen, they felt forced to harsh, wholesale measures on account of the gigantic problem of expansion they were facing. Civilization at stake in the provinces forced the fight with the gaucho. The Indians and the white oppressors are Nature's upper and nether millstones: between them agonizes the doomed gaucho. What an epic struggle: vast as the pampa; heroic; imaginative and inclusive, rather than narrowly literal; heir of a purely anonymous line of gaucho romances, sung out of the heart of men of action rather than composed for bookworms! How

---

31. Foreigners, especially Italians.

gripping is the clutch of Fate, amid all the writhings of passionate resistance: not less inexorable than Homer's or the blood-lust of the *Niebelungenlied!*

None will deny the simplicity of the poem. Nor can the modesty of the minstrel be assailed, for his pride is in his "calling" of *payador,* not in himself as an individual. Few and far-between are the verses that describe his own status or achievements. He succeeds from the start in throwing the light upon the class he sings of, and breaks his instrument in flinders rather than court our favor.[32] He will be content to be nothing, if only his story lives. This quality is surely epic.[33] So much is Hernández, Martín Fierro, and so much is Martín, Hernández, that I am hardly sure whether I am speaking of the author or of his hero. Both Lugones[34] and Rojas[35] state that the poet was regularly called "Martín Fierro."

Martín Fierro is the culmination of all the gaucho literary production: the supreme expression of a life which, like Troy, "was." No other work of the class claims so much for itself, nor has any other as complete justification. An *a fortiori* is useful here. *Martín Fierro* is more serious than either *Santos Vega* or *Fausto.* But these two were the best of all the considerable gaucho narrations up to and including their year of publication. Hence *Martín Fierro* is, beyond doubt, the work to be reckoned with. Gutiérrez and other prominent writers coming after Hernández, betook themselves to the novel and the drama, as to fields not completely worked. Obligado is the only notable exception to the abandonment of lyric, and his *Santos Vega* is worked-over folklore, not firmly knit relation.

This poem of *Martín Fierro,* though aesthetically satisfying and historically true, though written by one whose mastery of the language must, I think, be admitted, has not yet been universally recognized. *Martín Fierro* has received great praise in all the South American countries, probably all that could be expected where jealousy and self-aggrandizement are common. It is much appreciated in Spain. That it has not conquered the rest of the western world is because of the comparative inconspicuousness of its scene, and the comparative ignorance of Spanish in nations outside the Hispanic group, until

---

32. *Ida,* XIII.

33. Article on *The Epic,* in *Universal Encyclopedia.*

34. *Op. cit.,* 179.

35. *Op. cit.,* 447.

recent days. I roundly affirm that its value is great, and will presently show in what that value is to be permanent.

And yet, it cannot escape criticism! Three sources of criticism may be noted as typical. Mitre was a contemporary. His objection has been mentioned. As an example of the second type, we may take *Nosotros,* an influential Buenos Aires monthly, which printed some years ago a symposium of the judgment of prominent literary and professional figures, as to the merits of Hernández' poem.[36] In the comments of some is heard a hostile note. One writer, with superb irony, suggested that all Argentine histories be re-written in gaucho language. For instance, were the untimely death of the jurisconsult Moreno to be related, the writer should say, instead of *Moreno murió,* or *expiró,* or *falleció: Moreno cantó pa el carnero!*[37] Hurled with intent to kill, such bolts failed of the mark. Hernández rightly let his gauchos speak for themselves.

However, another charge in *Nosotros* is more weighty. This is, that Hernández has not given true epic grandeur to his hero. Martín, it is urged, is a boozing, quarrelsome, knifing singer of creole jingles! His story is more than full of bar-room brawls. His associates are coarse, unlettered, and violent cowboys, and slatternly, bovine women. The previous charge was superficial, while this is directed at the spirit—nay, the *raison d'être* of the work. Let us console ourselves with the reflection that the same charge has often been made before, in the history of literature, with as little justification. The principal objection to the death-scenes in *Martín Fierro* and kindred works, seems to lie in the fact that the killing is not done with refinement, in the style of

à la fin de l'envoi, je touche!

As to the unfitness of Martín and his associates, this is beside the mark if in them there was an epic ideal, and in their lives an epic struggle.

When Calixto Oyuela, the noted Argentine poet, says *Martín Fierro* is not an epic poem,[38] we cannot do less than consider his charges, for this third type of criticism is the most authoritative. He says the theme should be of a national or collective character. But what was ever a *payador* like Martín, if not a representative, and does not every second

---

36. June, July, and August of 1913.
37. Parodying a verse in *Ida,* VII: a gaucho locution referring to the death agony.
38. In Notes to his *Antología Poética Hispano-Americana,* Book III, Vol. 2, 1110–1132.

line speak for *all* the creoles? Say what Oyuela will, the *Fierro* period was one of origins; the true origin of the republic as it now exists, the origin of expansion, the origin of popular reforms. If this is not national, the present writer would like to know what is.

But, he continues, the hero is a gaucho, and the gauchos are a rather degenerate class, already showing signs of *Moreirismo* (cf. what was said in Chap. II, of the novel *Juan Moreira*) and general outlawry. If a gaucho epic could have been written, its hero would have been Santos Vega. Does literature about real degenerates live forever, or, to limit the question, does it survive long in these modern days? Santos Vega lives on, as is proper, in Argentine lyrics, for he was a singer. Martín Fierro lives as a national type, in the supreme narrative poem of Argentina, for he was primarily a man of action, a pampa "hero."

The method, Oyuela tells us, has no serenity, for the epic elements are intermingled with the lyric, and so (presumably) the harmony of the whole is impaired. I have already tried to meet this objection. This is not the first instance of such intermingling. Ker[39] points to the Pheaecian episode in the *Odyssey*, as an interlude apparently unwarranted by the plot of the epic. Then he shows how the epic grandeur of Ulysses has room for this lyricism and how his character and adventures explain it.

The language is severely handled, it is hard to say just why, when Oyuela professes to be so thrilled by it. "Vulgarisms," in the Spanish sense of cheap, tawdry phrases, are alleged. *Correct* and *incorrect* grammatical forms, says Oyuela, are mingled. Strange, in *the* poem of the common people!

Oyuela's most energetic attack is directed against the author. The point he seeks to make is that Hernández was not so much an inspired poet as a propagandist. It is based on his letters to his publishers and his "forewords." But all the world knows how the cool, formal statement of a writer, especially to his publishers, or to a public whom he addresses *ex cathedra* may differ from the message kindled by the vital spark that animates his verse.

On the other hand, Oyuela has glowing words of commendation for certain episodes, which have been studied in these pages. What is rather curious, is that he admits the presence of epic elements, as we have seen. The adjective "magnificent" is requisitioned! Part II, which disappoints many critics, is eulogized for certain superiorities over Part I. The work is styled an "admirable example," a "moving tragedy,

---

39. *Op. cit.*, 88 ff.

full of power and character," and Hernández is declared to "identify himself with the feelings and nature of the gauchos!" These expressions are surprising on the lips of one who declared that Hernández was too far above the gaucho class to write a gaucho epic.

Clearly, the merit of *Martín Fierro* triumphs in the minds of even its most formidable critics.

Apparently what is needed for the right appraisal of *Martín Fierro* is a right perspective. Then criticism will not attempt to explain away the sordid and mean, the standards differing from our own, but will acclaim the epic features discerned through and in spite of these.

Defective the work is. *La Vuelta* is too long. Not even the "age of Christ"[40] excuses thirty-three cantos! Its introductory strophes are bombastic at times. The careers of Viscacha and Picardía are overloaded. Unfortunately, too, the poet seems to have difficulty in stopping, in XXXII and XXXIII! Rojas notes that most of the characters have hardly a speaking part, and regrets that there is no substantial feminine personality.[41] More serious, at least from the critic's point of view, is the lack of an argument of major proportions. The argument is mainly chronological. When we remember the curious and intriguing contrasts in the *Cantar del Cid*, we cannot deny that with epic simplicity there may go also an absorbing and well-developed plot. I do not attempt to gloss over this failure of Hernández. He produced a work of epic dimensions, but he was not a colossus. His genius, it seems to me, is revealed in this, were all else to be forgotten: he provokes comparison, in many vital respects, with the old Spanish romancers and authors of the *cantares de gesta*. It is curious that at the two extremes, that of the romancers and this of the nineteenth century, should be found the same robust, if often primitive type. Supremely artistic the *gesta* are not, nor is *Martín Fierro;* but profoundly ethical, fundamentally sound, and unwaveringly manly and noble, both products are. To these excellent qualities, I suppose the sage of Weimar would add that of "striving": certainly the struggle is insistent and imposing in both the ancient and the modern *gesta*. And when we have forgotten the horror in the *Infantes de Lara* and the bloody scenes in *Martín Fierro,* we shall still

---

40.   *Estos son 33 cantos*
                                   Que es la mesma edá de Cristo.

                                 —*Vu,* XXXIII

41. *Op. cit.,* 496.

be remembering, probably, the *hidalguía,* the loyalty (e.g., of Fierro to Cruz), the sobriety in thought, the *common sense* that inform them.

Hernández also reminds us vividly at times of Calderón and other great figures of Spain's literary apogee. The concepts and language of a passage in *Ida,* XIII are reminiscent of those in the famous soliloquy of Segismundo in Act I of *La Vida es Sueño,* with its refrain, *Y teniendo yo más alma, tengo menos libertad?*

Segismundo contrasts with himself, in the following order:

I. Birds

And with more soul,
Shall I have less liberty?

II. Animals

And I, with better instincts,
Shall I have less liberty?

III. Fishes

And I, with more will,
Shall I have less liberty?

IV. The Brook

And I, with more life,
Shall I have less liberty?

Fierro has the following contrasts (in the order cited), suggesting a refrain:

I. Flowers

But to man God gave more
When he gave him a heart.[42]

---

42. *Pero al hombre le dió más*
     Cuando le dió el corazón.

II. Light, Wind, etc.

But he gave the Christian more
When he gave him reason.[43]

III. Birds

He gave man a greater treasure
In a speaking tongue.[44]

IV. Wild Beast

What less would he give man
Than courage to defend himself?[45]

Observe that the *menos* of Hernández occurs but once. The heated repetition of the rhetorical questions of Segismundo is more effective than the sad refrain of Martín Fierro. Of course the yearning for liberty is in Fierro, but this passage only implies it.

Again, there is the famous advice of father to son in *El Alcalde de Zalamea* (Jornada Segunda, Sc. XXIII), reminding us of Fierro's praiseworthy counsels to his sons in *Vu*, XXXII.

Through the literature of the golden age in Spain runs the vein of Gongorism. Perhaps after considering the above citations, the reader will not be surprised to find this tendency in Hernández.

Sepan que olvidar lo malo
También es tener memoria.

—*Vu*, XXXIII

is a phrase Góngora would not have scorned.[46]

---

43.   *Pero más le dió al cristiano*
       Al darle el entendimiento.
44.   *Le dió al hombre más tesoro*
       Al darle una lengua que habla.
45.   *¿Qué menos le daría al hombre*
       Que el valor pa su defensa?
46. Let them know that to forget the bad is also to have a memory.

José M. Salaverría calls attention in *El Poema de la Pampa* to the presence of such concepts in the *payada*, and throughout the poem.[47] His study supports the thesis that the poem is a genuinely popular Spanish work. He grasps at once the picaresque side of Viscacha—"he is just a *pícaro* of Mateo Alemán"—and of Picardía.[48]

Ascending in the literary scale, the fact that Hernández wrote a Part II, like Cervantes, leads Salaverría to say[49] that if in the book there is to be seen the influence of any literary work, it surely is that of *Don Quijote*. At the end of Part I he says Hernández parodies a phrase of Cervantes, when the latter paid his respects to his literary competitors.[50]

> *When this gaucho has sung.*
> *Pues naides ha de cantar*
> *Cuando este gaucho cantó.*
>
> —*Ida*, XIII

And (continues this critic) he says, as Don Quijote might have said aforetime:[51]

> *No faltaban. . .*
> *Muchos que ya conocían*
> *La historia de Martín Fierro.*
>
> —*Vu*, XI

Salaverría is, I think, writing just here of resemblances which are hints, which make us say to ourselves, "Where did I read something like that before?" With the general trend of his argument it is impossible not to be in accord. Here is a fine sentence: "It is a book Catholic, noble, valiant, generous, with some stoical sadness, and some biting jests, drenched with popular humor."[52] On page 125, we read: "It is one of the few works of

---

47. *Op. cit.*, 124.
48. *Ibid.*, 115.
49. *Ibid.*, 122.
50.   *No one is to sing*
51.   *There were not lacking many who knew*
                The story of Martín Fierro.
52. *Ibid.*, 121–122.

genius of the Plata region;" in Chapter XII, there is a guarded prophecy concerning the fame it is destined to acquire.[53]

As to the degree and permanence of this fame the verdict may be dependent on conditions, but I confidently look to see these fulfilled. If it has been held in the past a literary treasure, if it is at least a partial epitome of what the Argentine soul experiences today, if it also speaks for tomorrow, then its universality is unassailable and it must be pronounced a great work. That it expresses at least partially the soul of the Argentina of today, I think most will agree. The Argentine heart is much the same as it was fifty years ago. (Its literature proves this.) Erection of sky-scrapers and installation of central-heating-plants will not make over the man who spends one day banking in the capital, and the ensuing thirty astride his *flete* on the pampa. Take the word of a teacher who has watched the genuine sons of Argentina for five years, and happens to be writing these lines. The gauchos live on in their sons and grandsons. The spirit of those who dominated the red men and wrestled with Nature, is not to be extinguished by courses in physics and history in the *Colegios Nacionales*. No; *Martín Fierro* pictures the life and soul of the modern Argentine, better than most contemporary works.

Its future fate need not give us concern as long as the Argentine Desert prints its "something unique" on the characters of all the sons of that fair land. Should the Pampa of yesterday and today be altered before tomorrow, the strife between the metropolitan government and the interior might still very conceivably be carried on for many generations. With both these elements eliminated, we still are faced by the temperament of the typical Argentine: sensuous, responsive, supersensitive on the point of honor, enduring, capable of immense suffering or of fiery conquest, "making love or war," says Fierro, "with a song."

"Defer to no one, lower than God," is yet another word of his. It does not require a great flight of fancy, to find a relation between this sentiment and certain administrative considerations which seem, in the teeth of an almost worldwide sentiment, to have swayed Argentina in the last few years. Some one will say that the above motto is Spanish. This is true; but the fact only strengthens the case, for if there is one thing certain, it is that the Spanish heritage will not fade out in Argentina.

---

53. *Ibid.*, 139–140.

Indeed, the gaucho fighting for his hearth, his *pago,* his patron, is the old Spaniard *redivivus,* who never cared who inhabited the next valley, but fought fiercely for the rights of his own.

But let us imagine both the physical surroundings so essential to this whole gaucho drama, and the temperamental inheritances with the social friction they entail, to have been blotted out. There would yet remain the historic gaucho tradition and its effects—tradition wafted in song from home to school, from theater to *tertulia,* from café to *pulpería.* If Fierro were eliminated from the Argentine blood, his constant reappearance in the popular mind would have great significance.

As long as Argentina exists; as long as there, and over all the earth, men have the key to unlock her literary treasures—so long will *Martín Fierro* continue to be held in honor.

Such, in varying phrase, is the tribute of Palma of Peru; Roxlo[54] of Uruguay; Cané, Rojas, García Velloso, Gálvez,[55] and Lugones of Argentina; Menéndez y Pelayo, Salaverría, and Unamuno of Spain.

Says Menéndez y Pelayo: "The breeze of the Argentine pampa blows through his verses, in which all the energy of primitive, unconquered passion breaks loose, to battle with that social machine which vainly seeks to repress the hero's impulses."[56]

Unamuno's appreciation of the poem is so spontaneous and so thoroughly Spanish that it must bring joy to every lover of *Martín Fierro*:

"In *Martín Fierro* epic and lyric elements are mingled, and, as it were, deeply interfused. Of all Spanish American things I know, it is the most profoundly Spanish. When the *payador* of the pampa, beneath some *ombú,* in the boundless calm of the desert or in the peaceful, starlit night, sings to his guitar the monotonous *décimas* of *Martín Fierro,* and the gauchos hear with emotion the poetry of their pampas, they will feel, without knowing it or being able to account to themselves for it, that from the unconscious deeps of their soul surge inextinguishable echoes of Spain, the mother country, echoes. . . which their forefathers

---

54. *Historia de la Literatura uruguaya,* II, 242: The greatest gaucho poem.

55. He represents a notable and numerous group of admirers of Hernández in the *Nosotros* articles.

56. El soplo de la pampa argentina corre por sus versos, en que estallan todas las energías de la pasión indómita y primitiva, en lucha con el mecanismo social que inútilmente comprime los ímpetus del protagonista.

—*Historia de la Poesía Hispano-Americana,* II, 473

bequeathed to them. *Martín Fierro* is the song of that Spanish warrior who, after having planted the cross in Granada, went to America to serve as the advance-guard of civilization and to clear the way through the desert."[57]

57. En *Martín Fierro* se compenetran y como se funden íntimamente el elemento épico y el lírico: *Martín Fierro es,* de todo lo hispanoamericano que conozco, lo más hondamente español. Cuando el payador pampero, a la sombra del ombú, en la infinita calma del desierto, o en la noche serena a la luz de las estrellas, entone, acompañado de la guitarra española, las monótonas décimas de *Martín Fierro,* y oigan los gauchos conmovidos la poesía de sus pampas, sentirán, sin saberlo, ni poder de ello darse cuenta, que les brotan del lecho inconsciente del espíritu, ecos inextinguibles de la madre España, ecos. . . que les legaron sus padres. *Martín Fierro* es el canto del luchador español que, después de haber plantado la cruz en Granada, se fué a América a servir de avanzada a la civilización y abrir el camino del desierto.

—*Revista Española,* 1894, No. 1.

A Note About the Authors

Henry A. Holmes was an American translator and scholar. After several years of living in Uruguay and Argentina, he became familiar with the works of José Hernández and the gaucho lifestyle he celebrated. Part translation, part scholarly work, *Martín Fierro: An Epic of the Argentine* (1923) was published as partial fulfillment of Holmes' PhD in Philosophy from Columbia University.

José Hernández (1834–1886) was an Argentine poet, journalist, and politician. Born on a farm in Buenos Aires Province, he was raised in a family of cattle ranchers. Educated from a young age, he became a newspaperman during the violent civil wars between Uruguay and Argentina through his support of the Federalist Party. He founded El Río de la Plata, a prominent newspaper advocating for local autonomy, agrarian policies, and republicanism. Towards the end of his life, he completed his extensive epic poem Martín Fierro, now considered a national treasure of Argentine arts and culture.

A Note from the Publisher

Spanning many genres, from non-fiction essays to literature classics to children's books and lyric poetry, Mint Edition books showcase the master works of our time in a modern new package. The text is freshly typeset, is clean and easy to read, and features a new note about the author in each volume. Many books also include exclusive new introductory material. Every book boasts a striking new cover, which makes it as appropriate for collecting as it is for gift giving. Mint Edition books are only printed when a reader orders them, so natural resources are not wasted. We're proud that our books are never manufactured in excess and exist only in the exact quantity they need to be read and enjoyed.

Discover more of your favorite classics with Bookfinity™.

- Track your reading with custom book lists.
- Get great book recommendations for your personalized Reader Type.
- Add reviews for your favorite books.
- AND MUCH MORE!

Visit **bookfinity.com** and take the fun Reader Type quiz to get started.

Enjoy our classic and modern companion pairings!

Classic & Modern

Printed in the USA
CPSIA information can be obtained
at www.ICGtesting.com
JSHW082358140824
68134JS00020B/2157